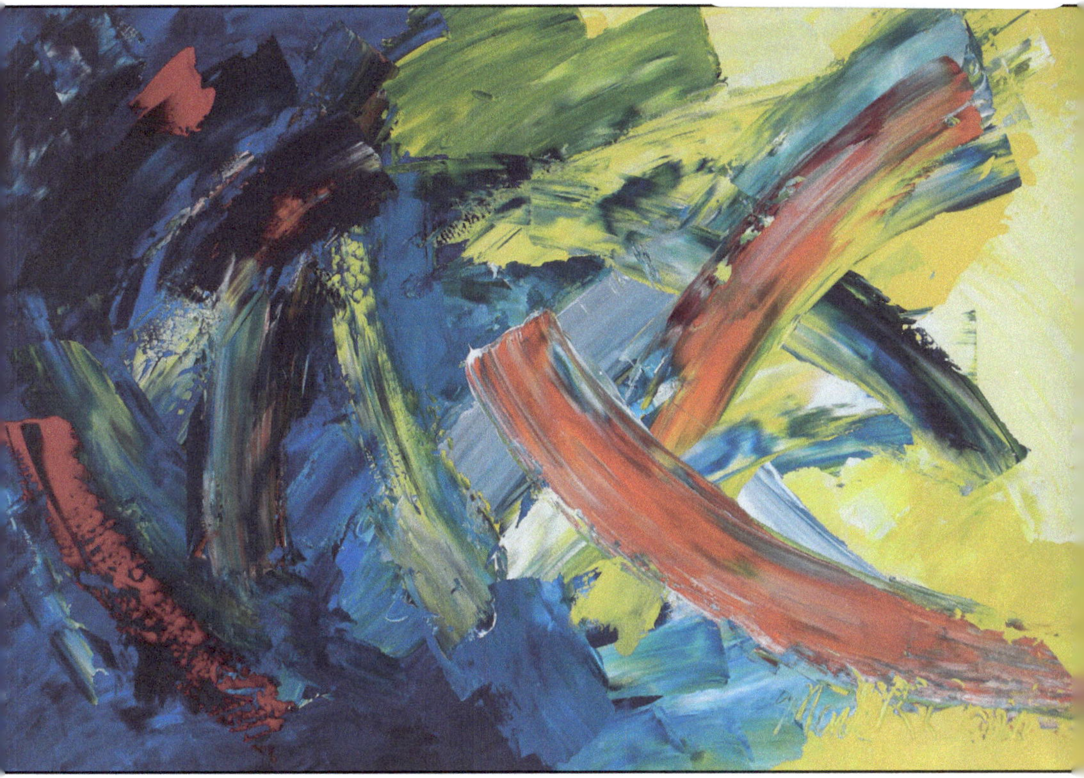

Endangered Photos

It takes a little time for green bales to turn golden. But in summer's 102-degree heat, that happens soon enough.

Unlike most fine art photographs where multiple prints exist, images in Mark Dahle's series of *Endangered Photos* are one-of-a-kind originals. Only one print is made by Mark Dahle from each image. If anything happens to the artwork, it is lost forever.

Besides hay bales, other subjects in Mark Dahle's *Endangered Photos* series include railroad ties, telephone poles, and train cars.

At the right:
Endangered Photos
Hay Bales #112

A Mark Dahle Portfolio

Endangered Photos

Hay Bales #112-222

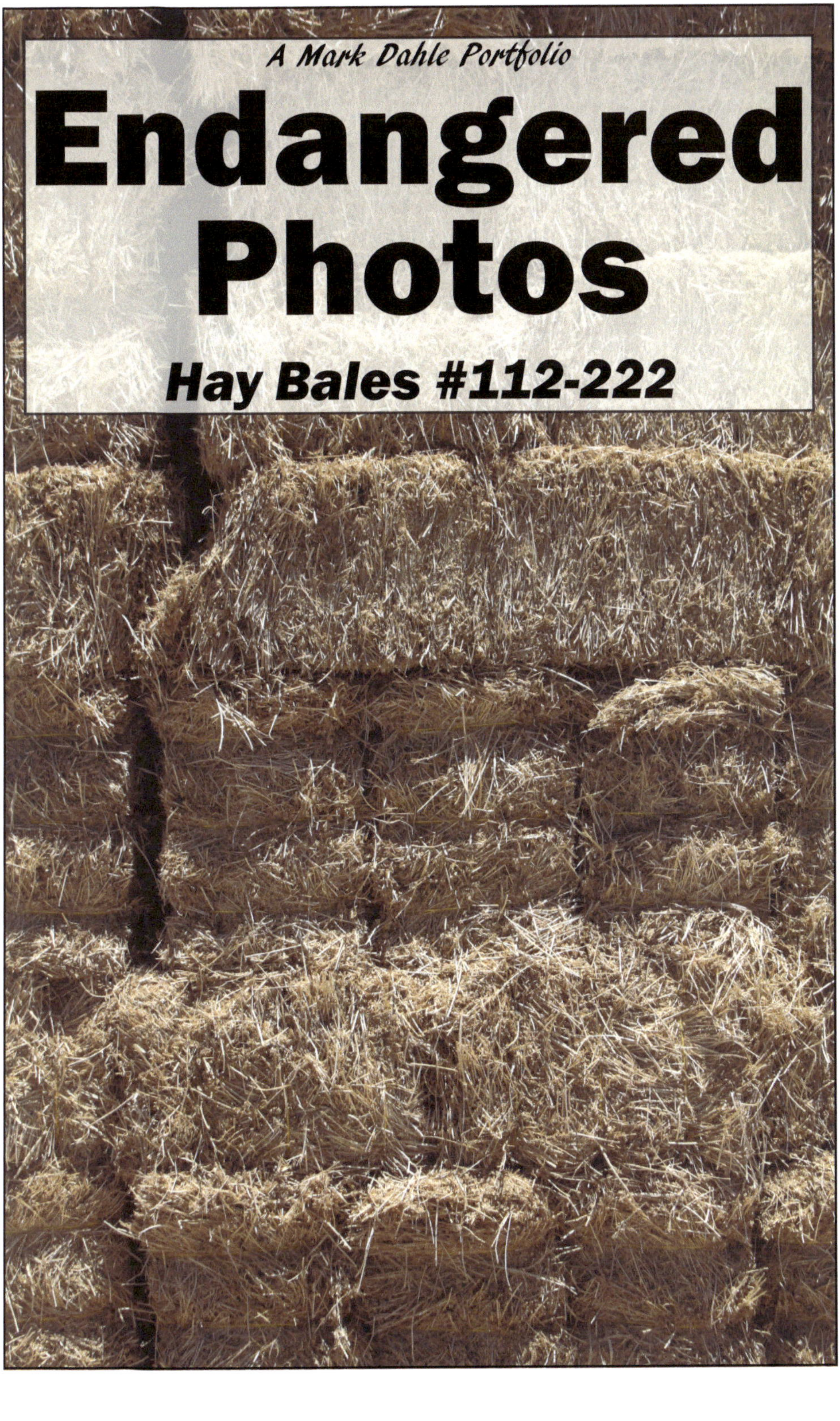

Mark Dahle Portfolios can be read in a few minutes and enjoyed for a lifetime.

This portfolio includes a photo of a brilliant 36 x 24 inch painting (at the right), 111 beautiful Endangered Photos *of hay bales, and a brief description of the* Endangered Photos *project.*

Photographs in this book may be available to collectors. See http://www.MarkDahle.com for more information and for previews of upcoming portfolios.

© Mark Dahle 2016. All rights reserved.

We do our best to create portfolios free of editing mistakes. But it's hard to catch everything. We reward people who report errors in any Mark Dahle portfolio. For details see MarkDahle.com/Typos.html or send an email to MarkDahle@aol.com with the subject line "Typos." Thanks!

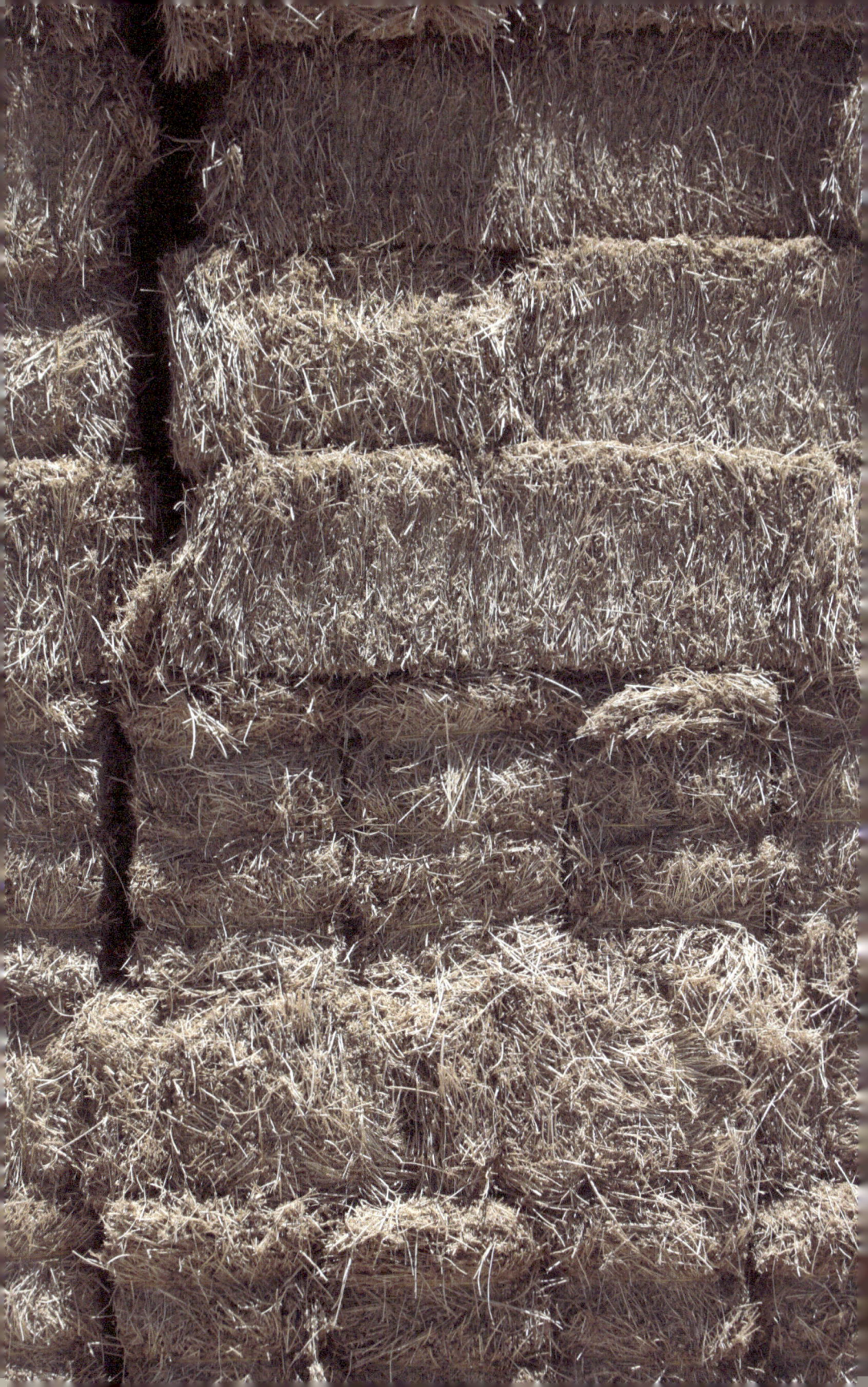

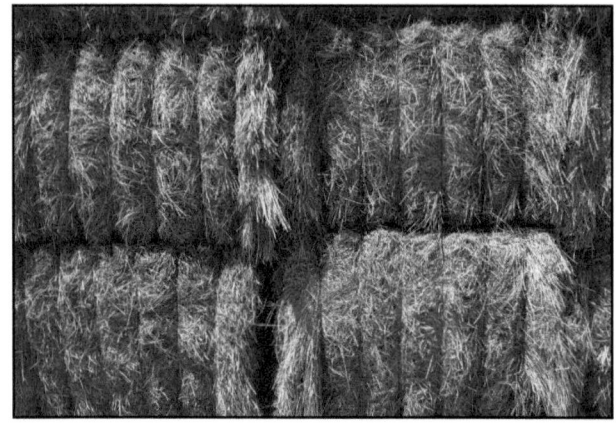

Endangered Photos:
Hay Bales
#113

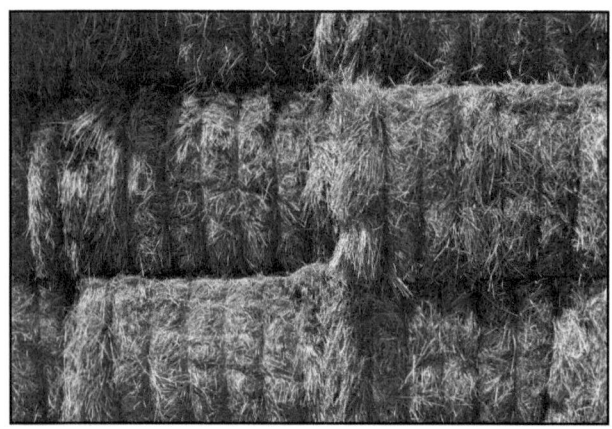

Endangered Photos:
Hay Bales
#114

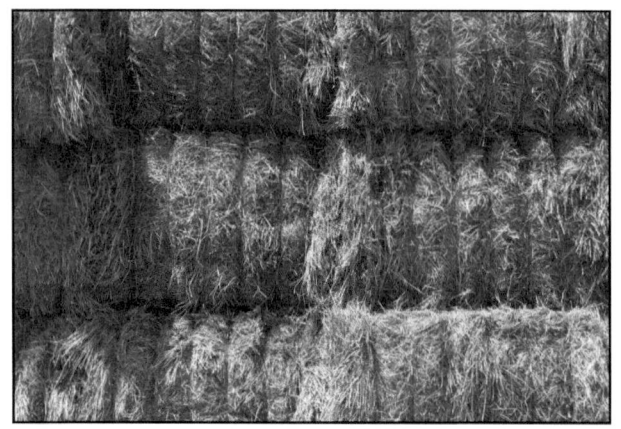

Endangered Photos:
Hay Bales
#115

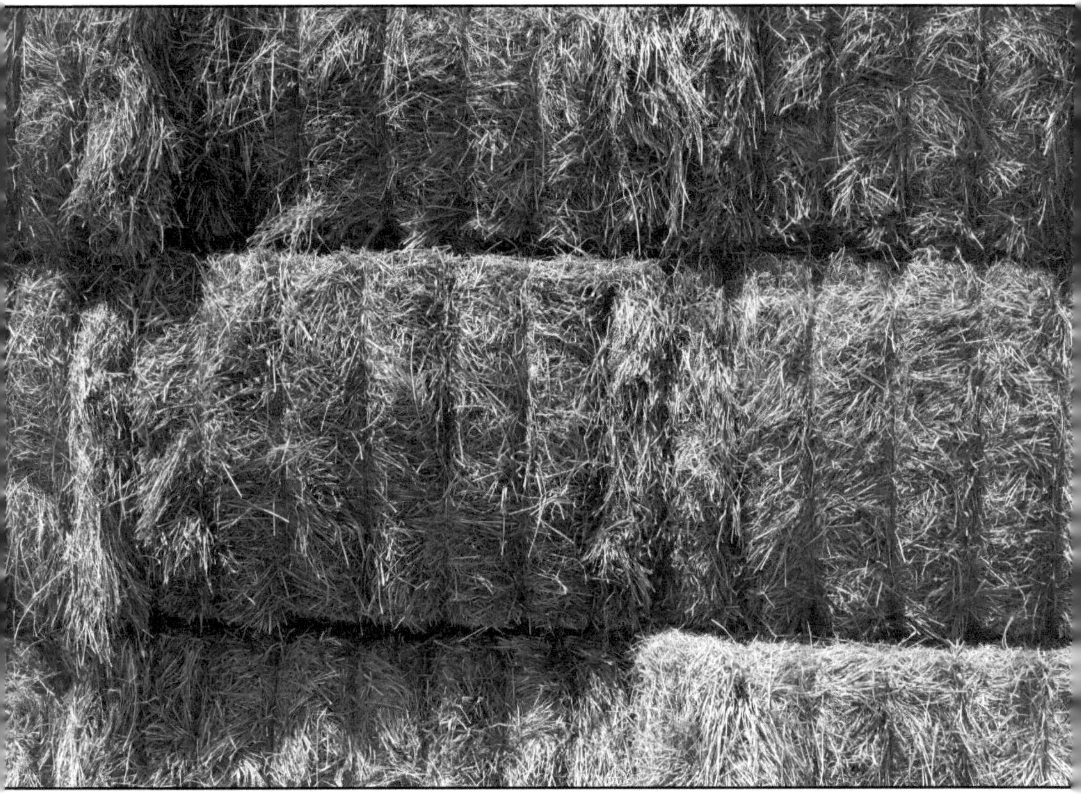

Endangered Photos: Hay Bales #116

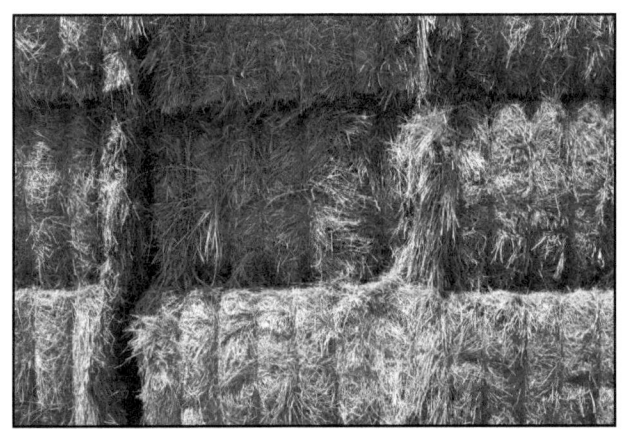

Endangered
Photos:
Hay Bales
#117

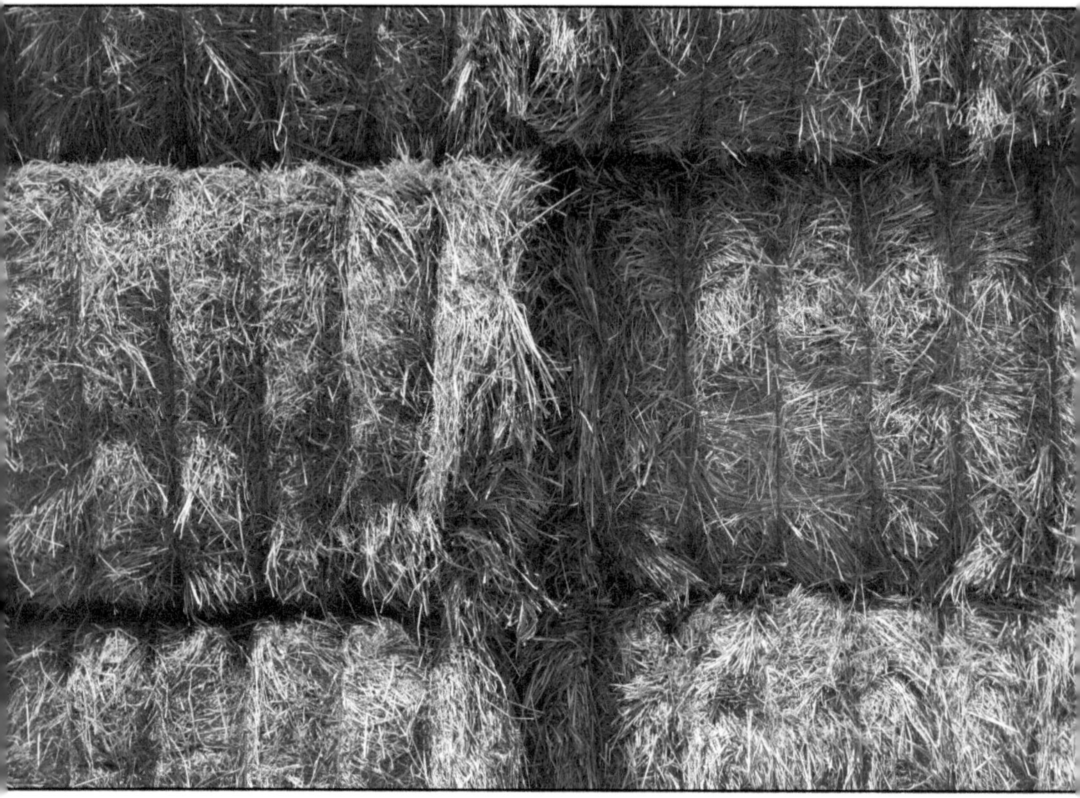

Endangered Photos: Hay Bales #118

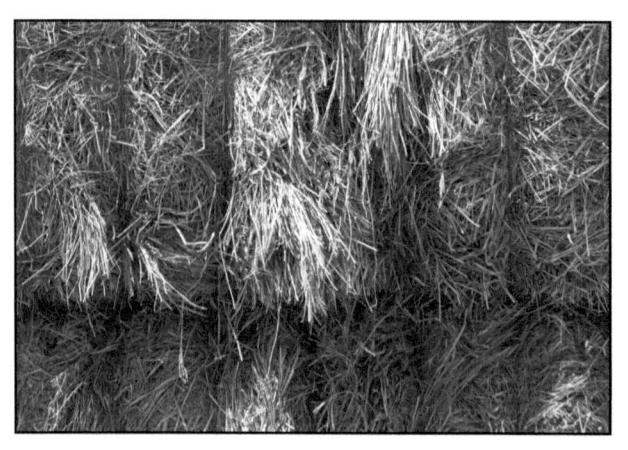

Endangered Photos: Hay Bales #119

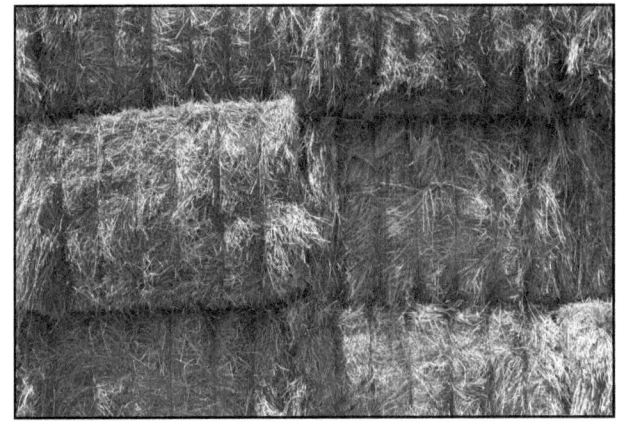

Endangered
Photos:
Hay Bales
#120

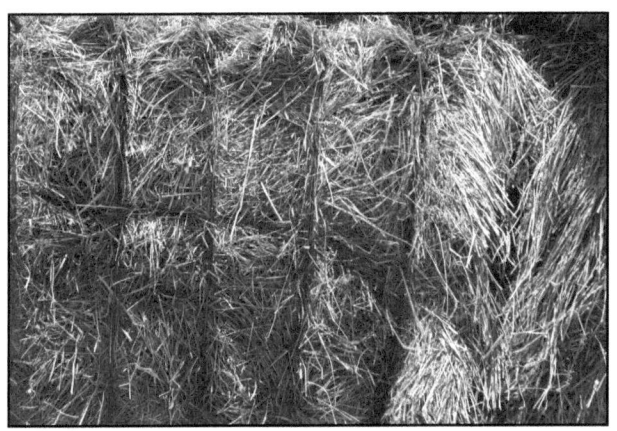

Endangered
Photos:
Hay Bales
#121

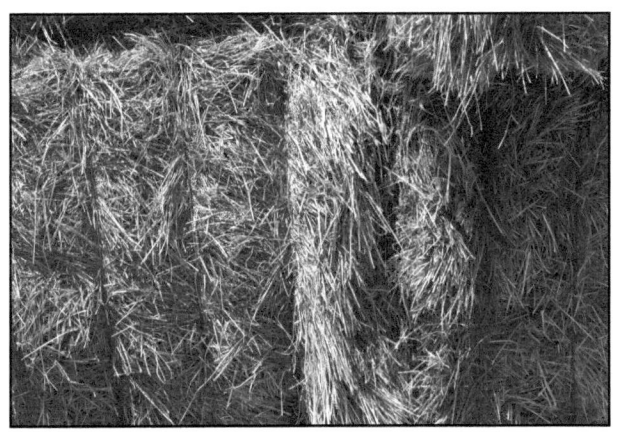

Endangered
Photos:
Hay Bales
#122

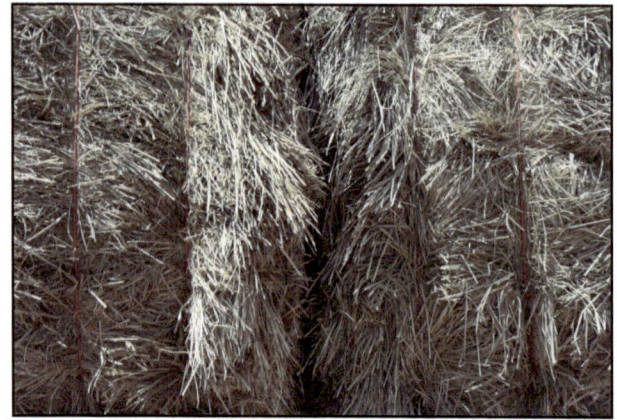

Endangered
Photos:
Hay Bales
#123

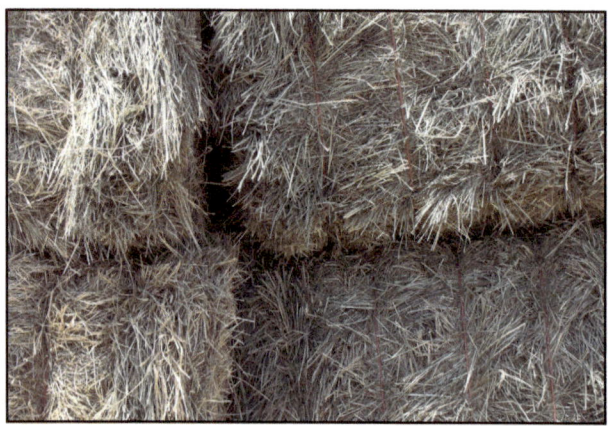

Endangered
Photos:
Hay Bales
#124

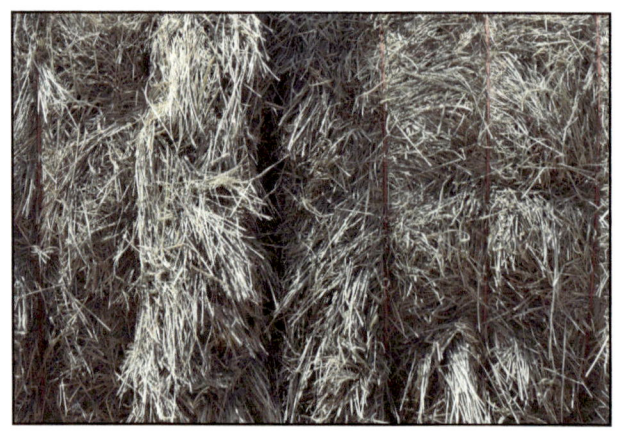

Endangered
Photos:
Hay Bales
#125

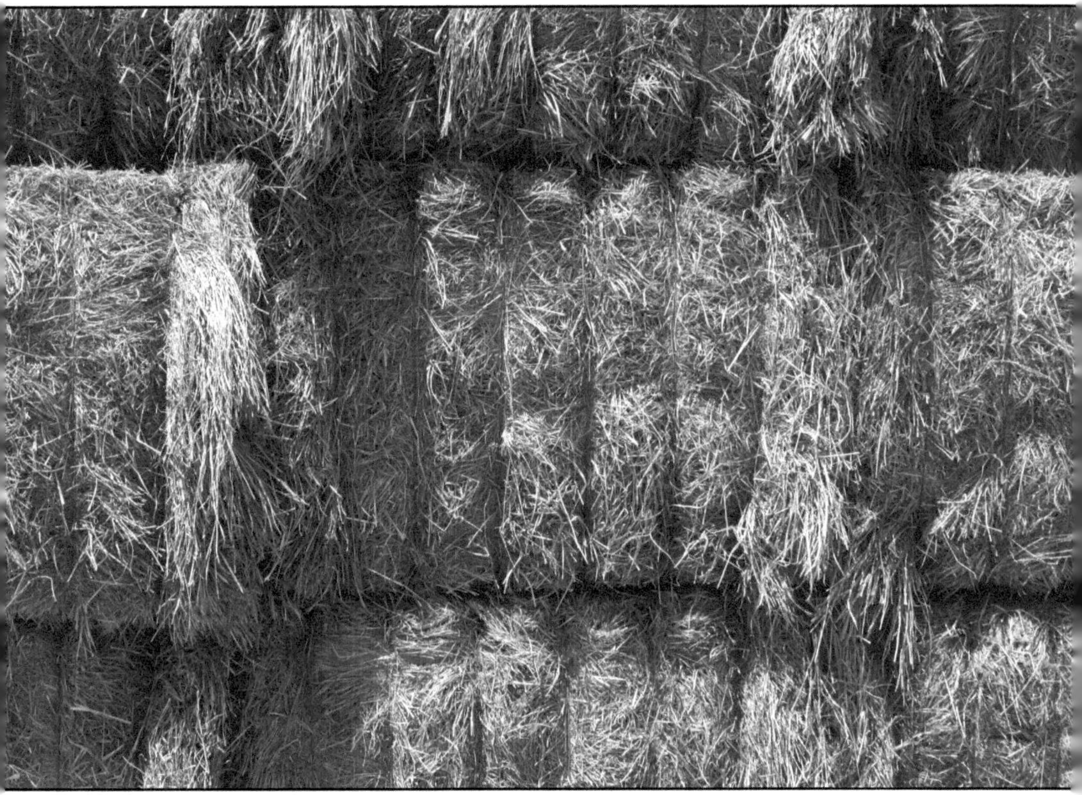

Endangered Photos: Hay Bales #126

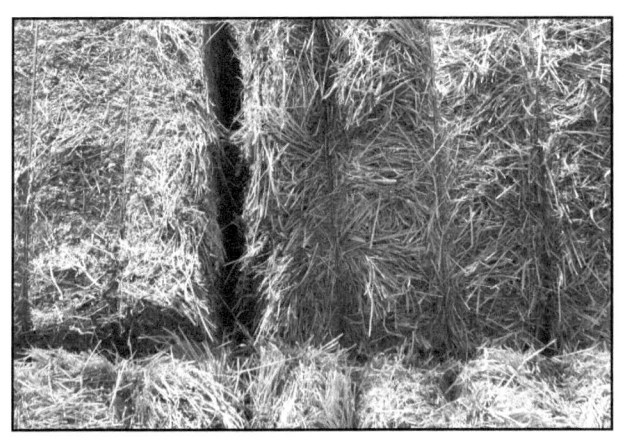

Endangered Photos: Hay Bales #127

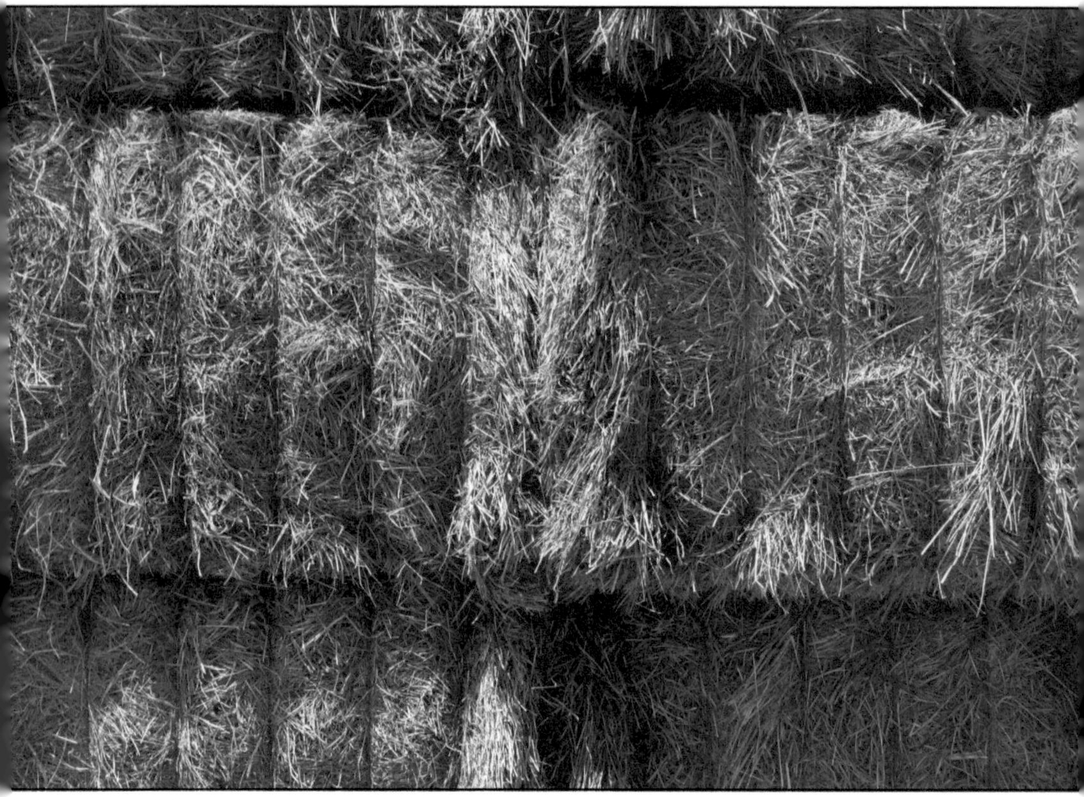

Endangered Photos: Hay Bales #128

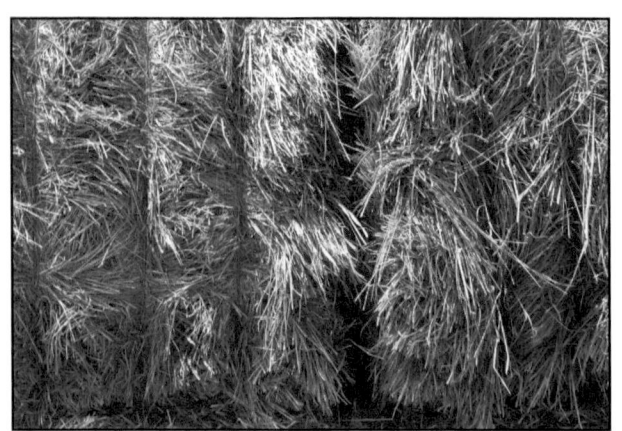

Endangered Photos: Hay Bales #129

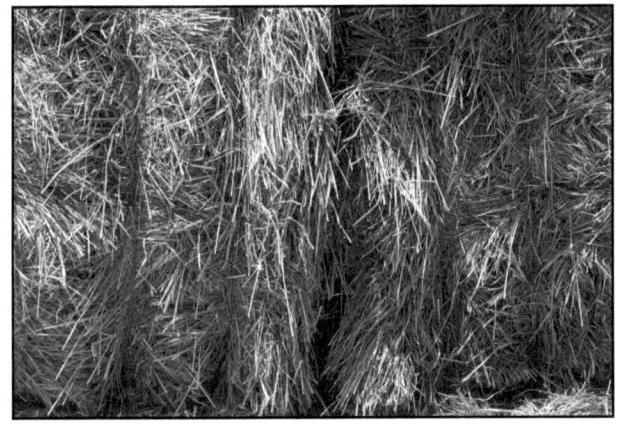

Endangered
Photos:
Hay Bales
#130

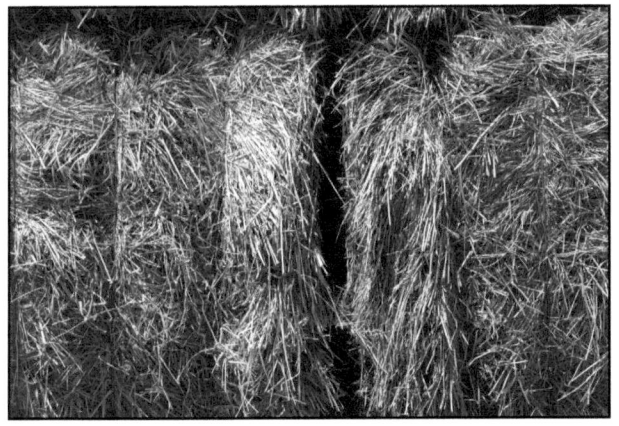

Endangered
Photos:
Hay Bales
#131

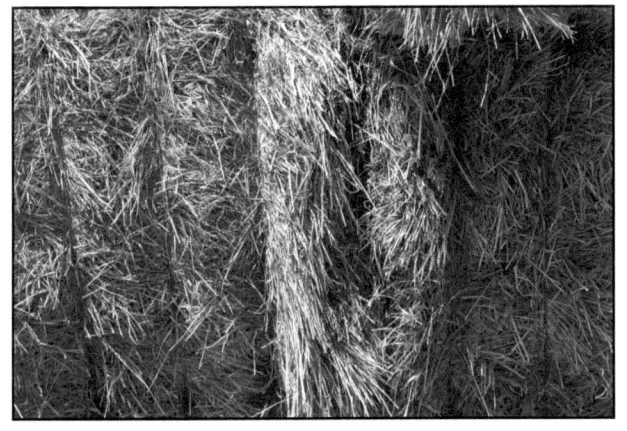

Endangered
Photos:
Hay Bales
#132

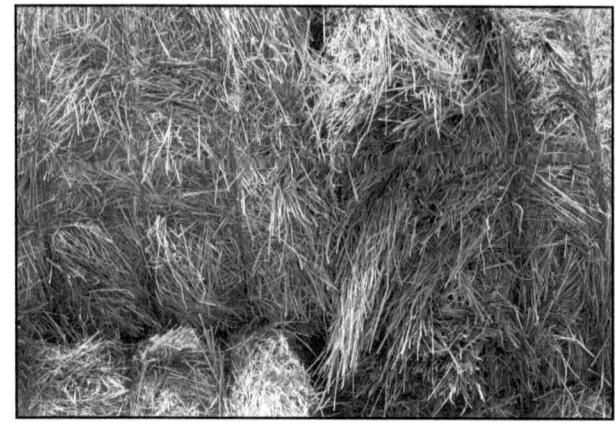

Endangered
Photos:
Hay Bales
#133

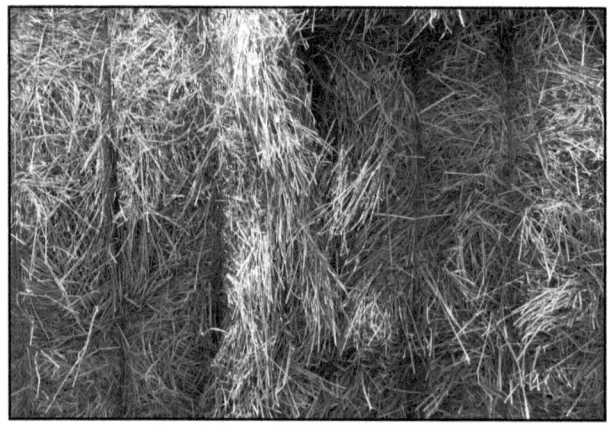

Endangered
Photos:
Hay Bales
#134

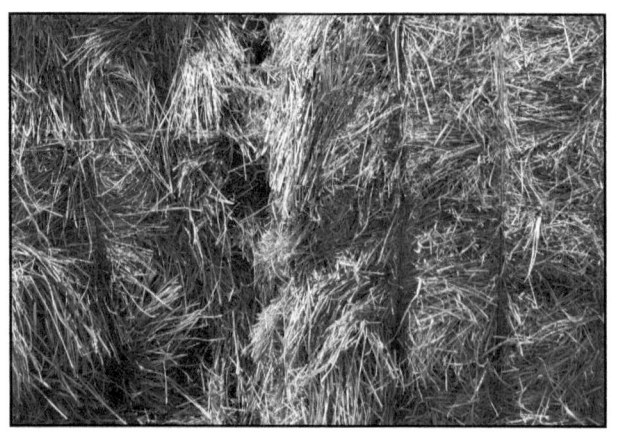

Endangered
Photos:
Hay Bales
#135

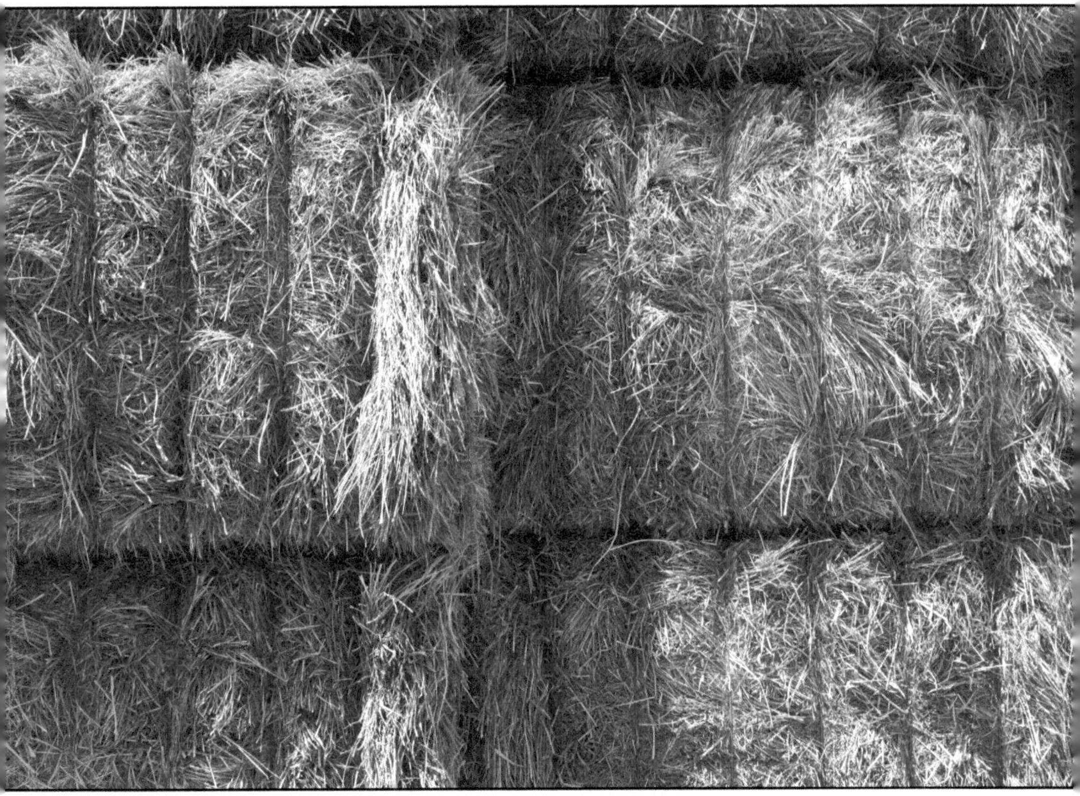

Endangered Photos: Hay Bales #136

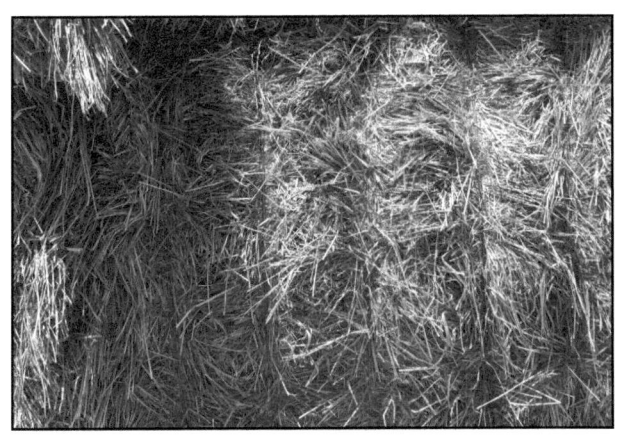

Endangered Photos: Hay Bales #137

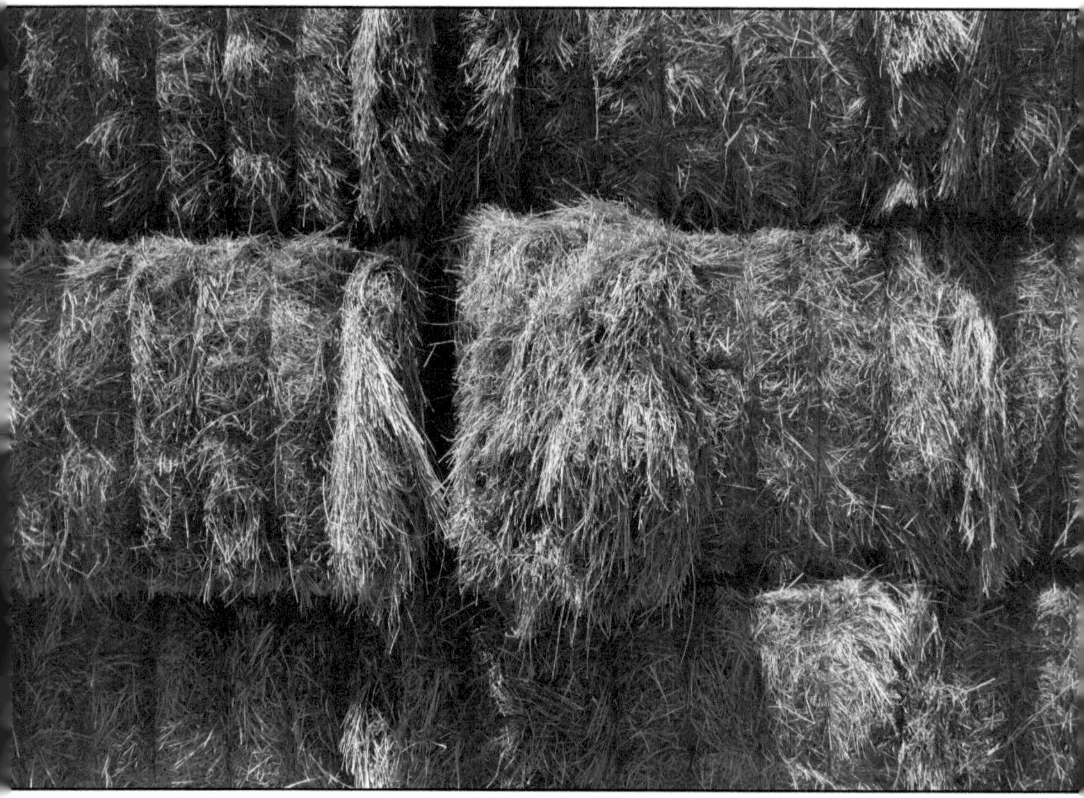

Endangered Photos: Hay Bales #138

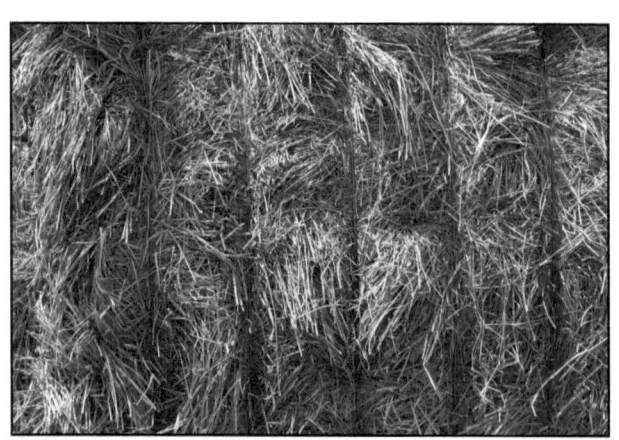

Endangered
Photos:
Hay Bales
#139

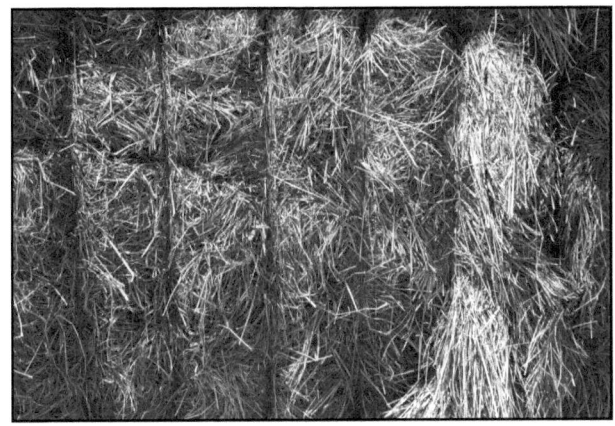

Endangered
Photos:
Hay Bales
#140

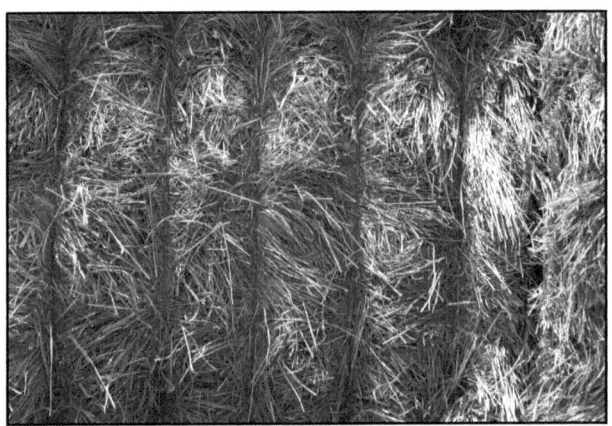

Endangered
Photos:
Hay Bales
#141

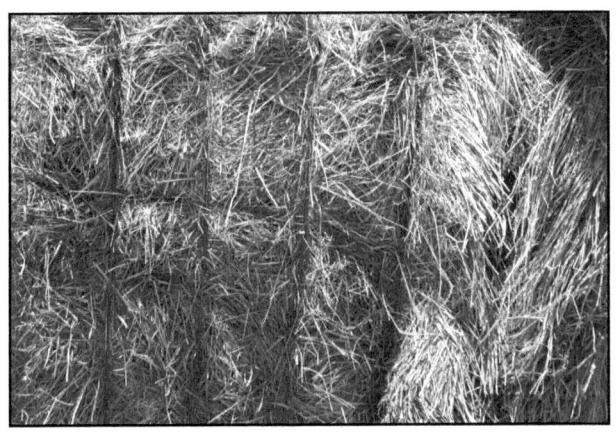

Endangered
Photos:
Hay Bales
#142

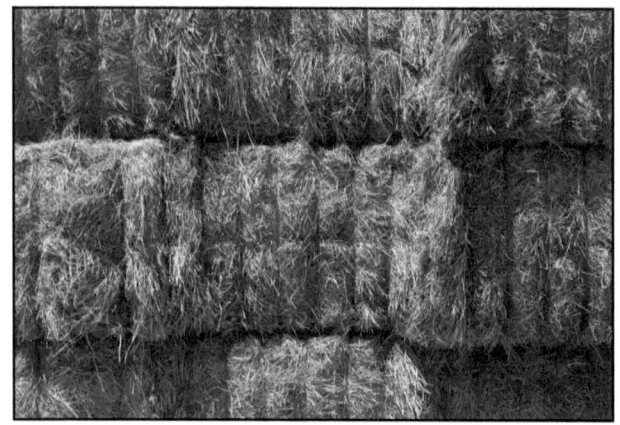

Endangered
Photos:
Hay Bales
#143

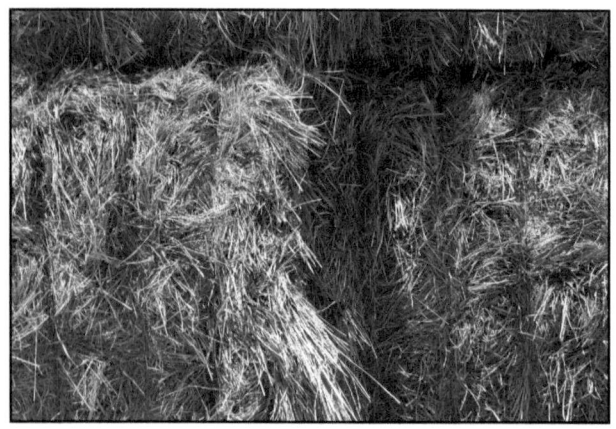

Endangered
Photos:
Hay Bales
#144

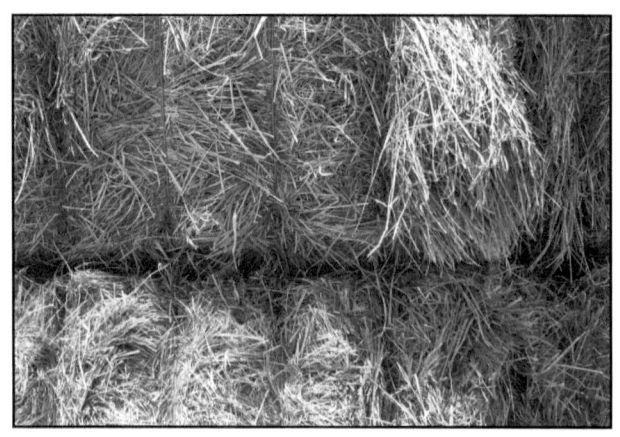

Endangered
Photos:
Hay Bales
#145

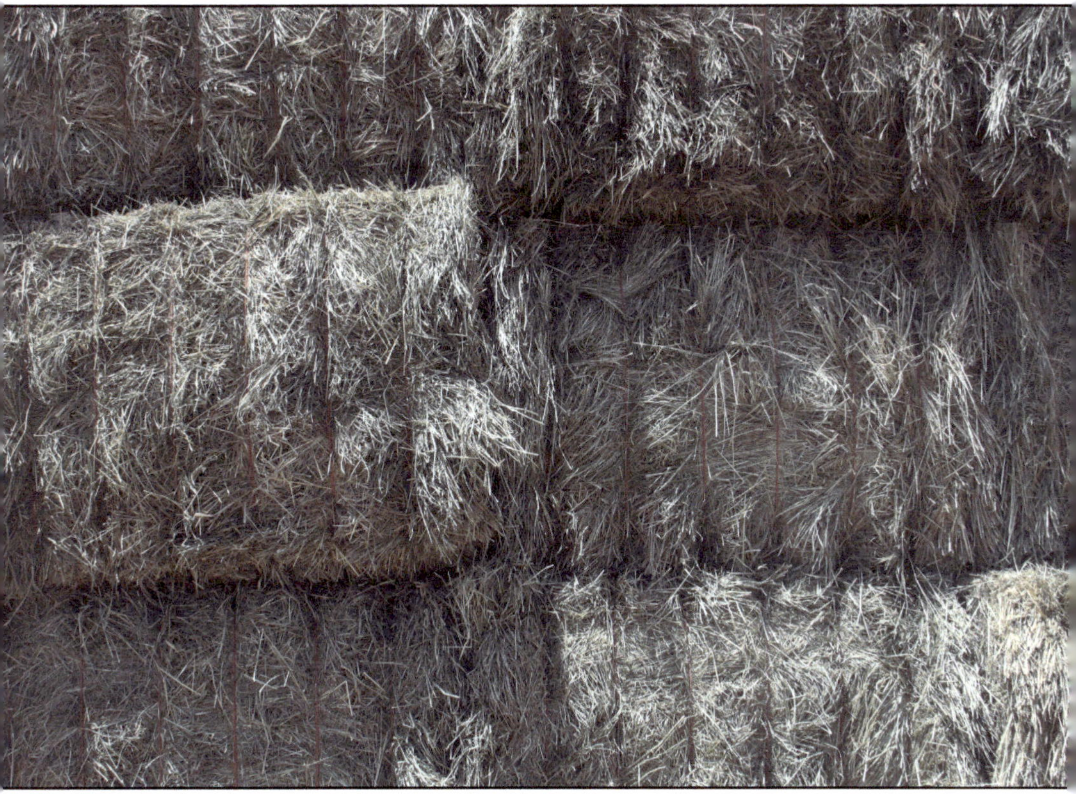

Endangered Photos: Hay Bales #146

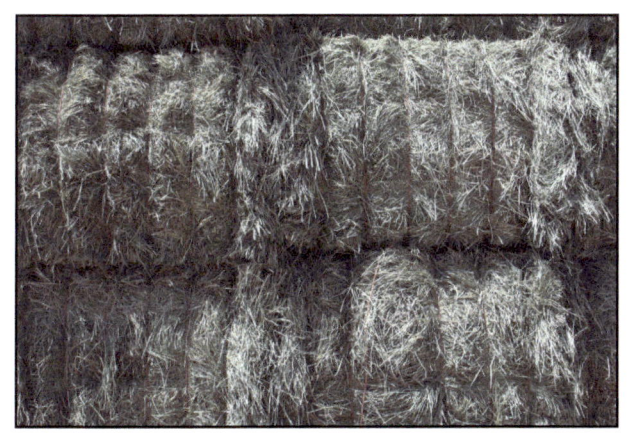

Endangered Photos: Hay Bales #147

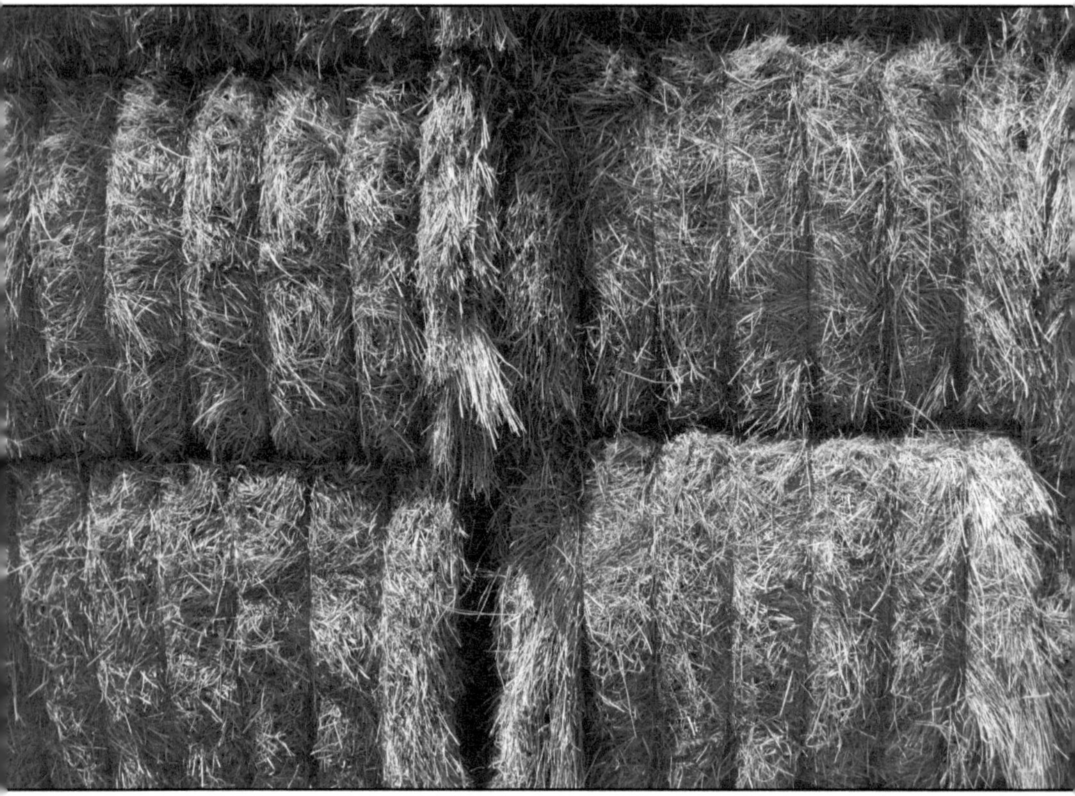

Endangered Photos: Hay Bales #148

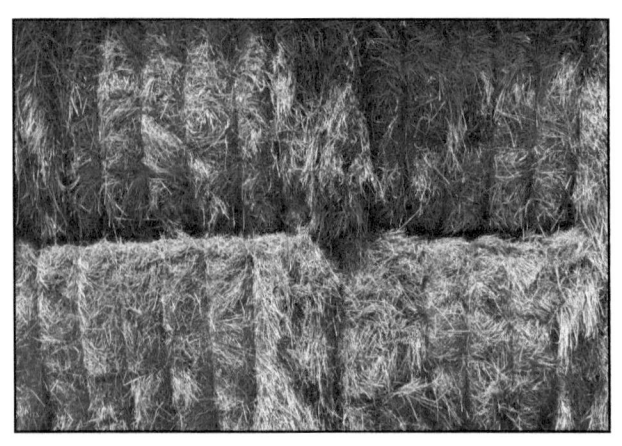

Endangered Photos: Hay Bales #149

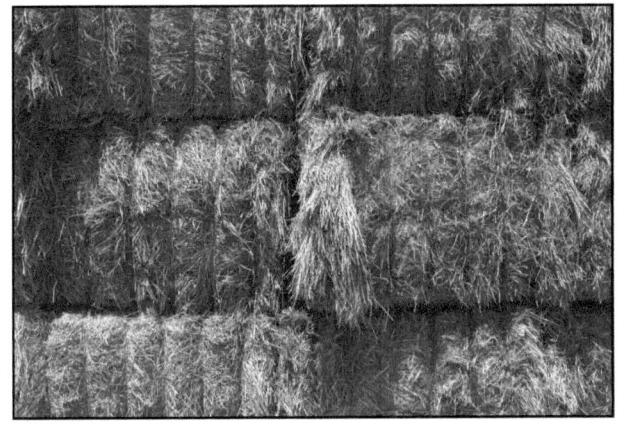

Endangered
Photos:
Hay Bales
#150

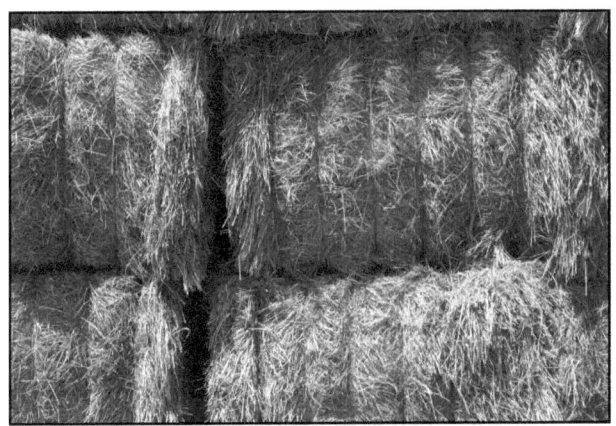

Endangered
Photos:
Hay Bales
#151

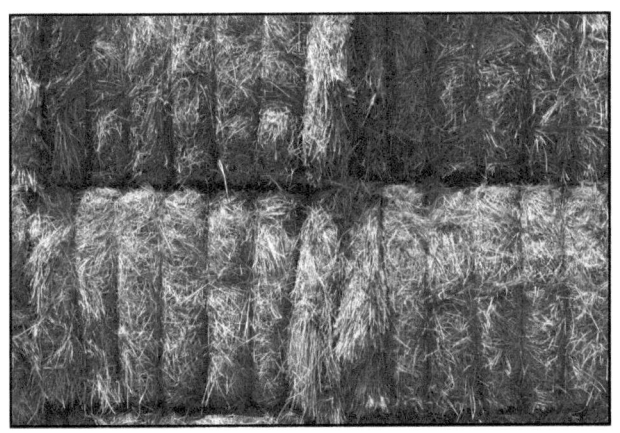

Endangered
Photos:
Hay Bales
#152

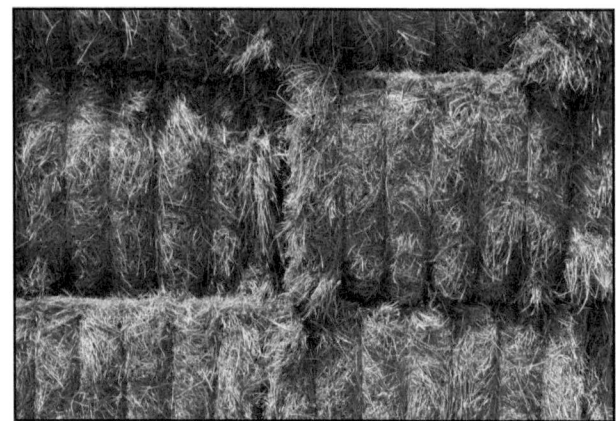

Endangered
Photos:
Hay Bales
#153

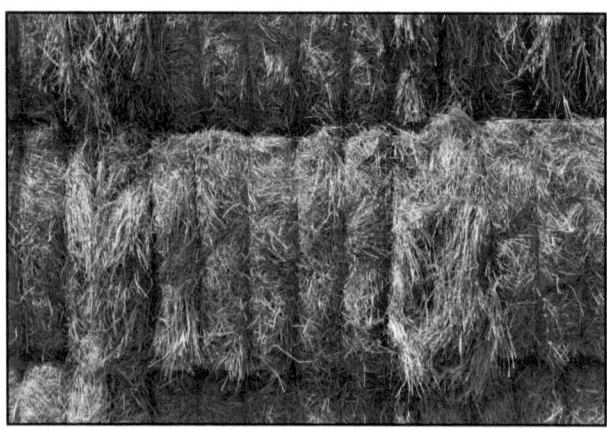

Endangered
Photos:
Hay Bales
#154

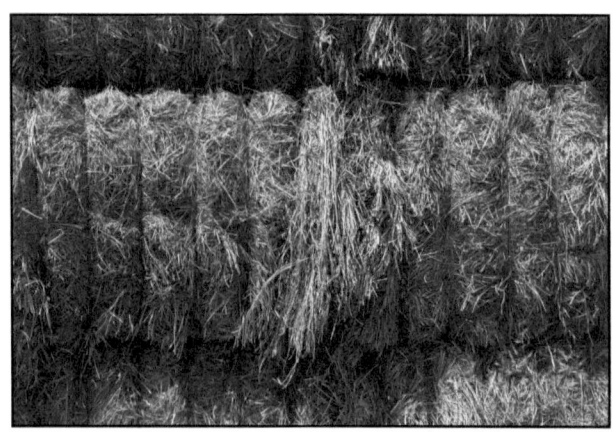

Endangered
Photos:
Hay Bales
#155

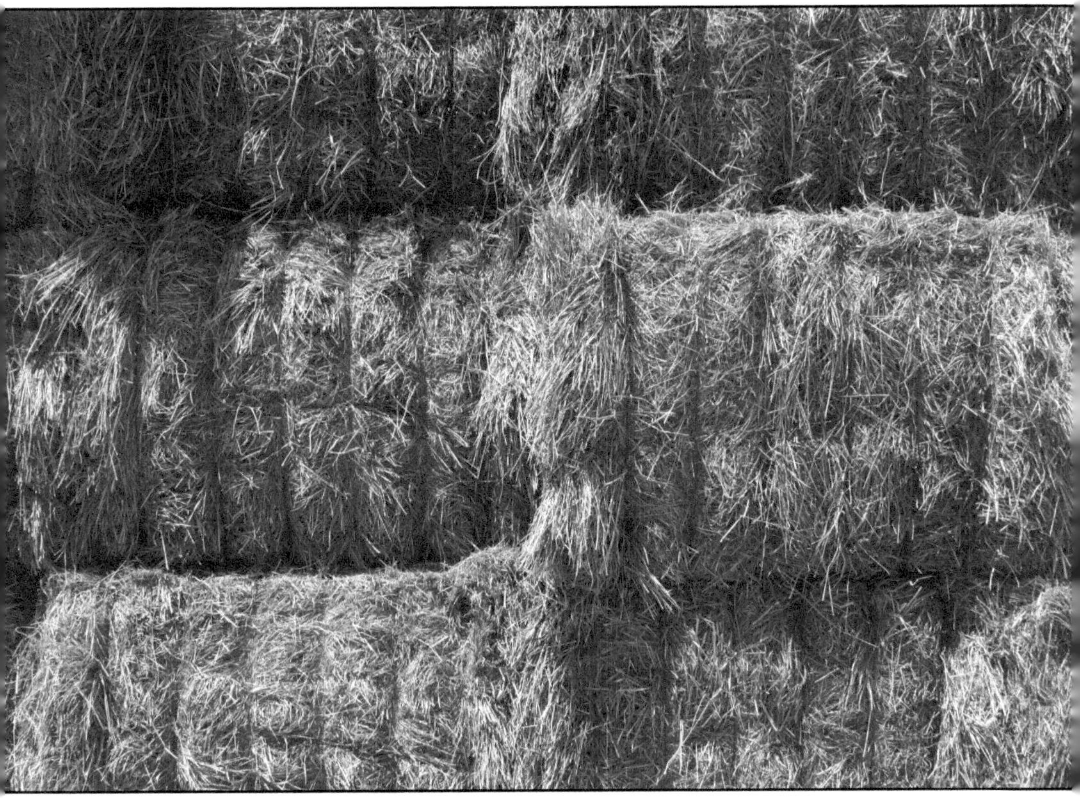

Endangered Photos: Hay Bales #156

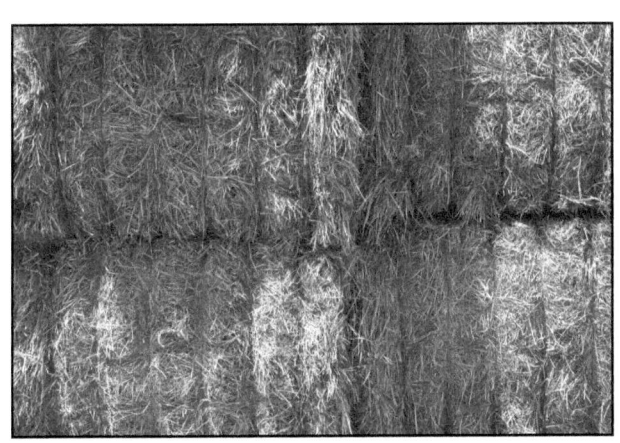

Endangered
Photos:
Hay Bales
#157

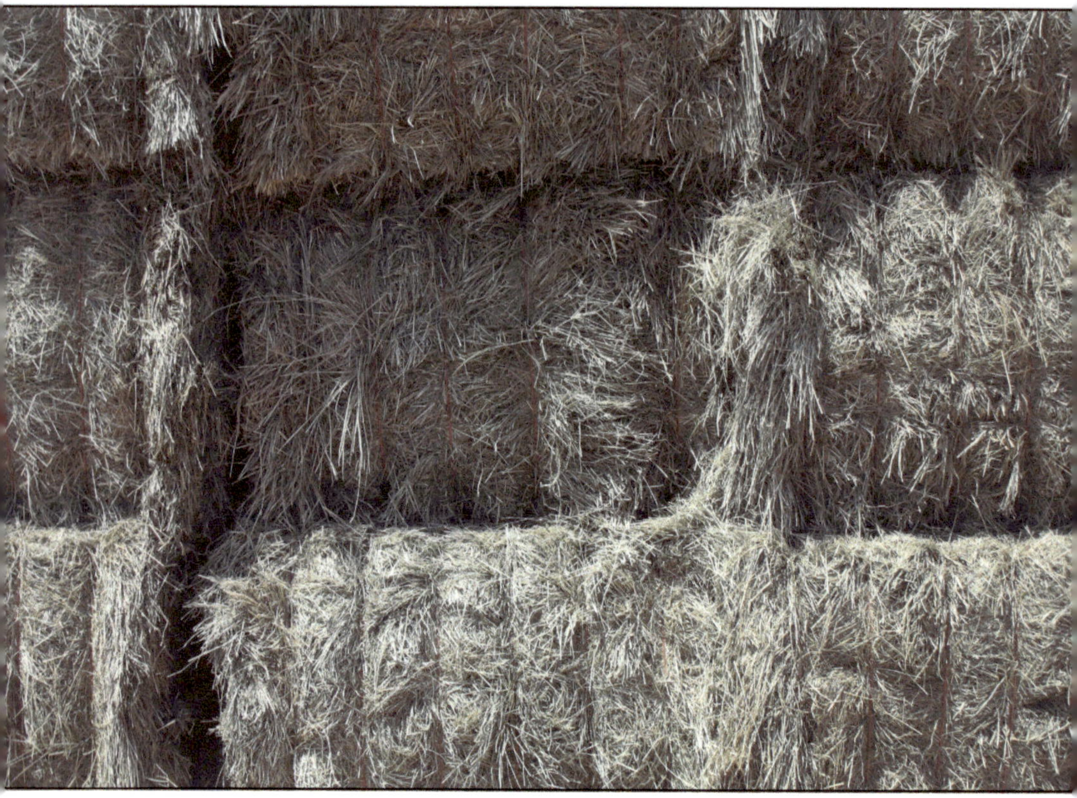

Endangered Photos: Hay Bales #158

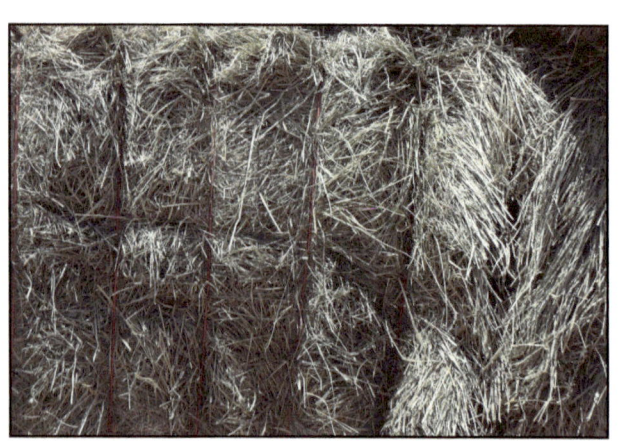

Endangered
Photos:
Hay Bales
#159

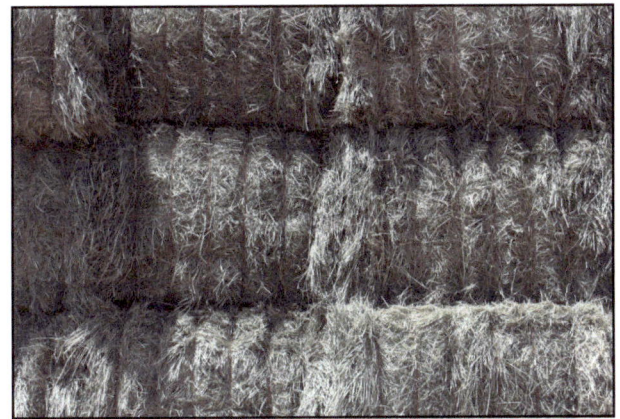

Endangered
Photos:
Hay Bales
#160

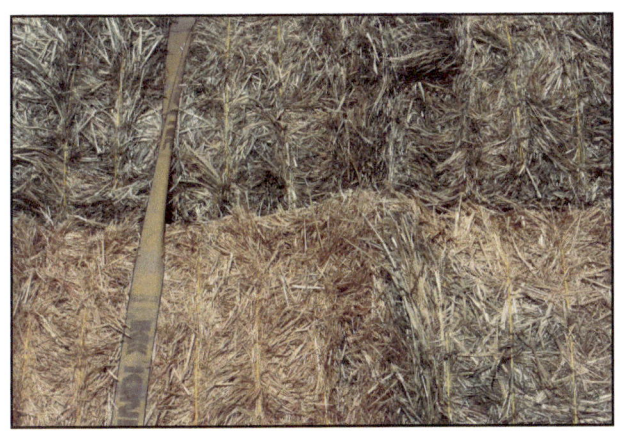

Endangered
Photos:
Hay Bales
#161

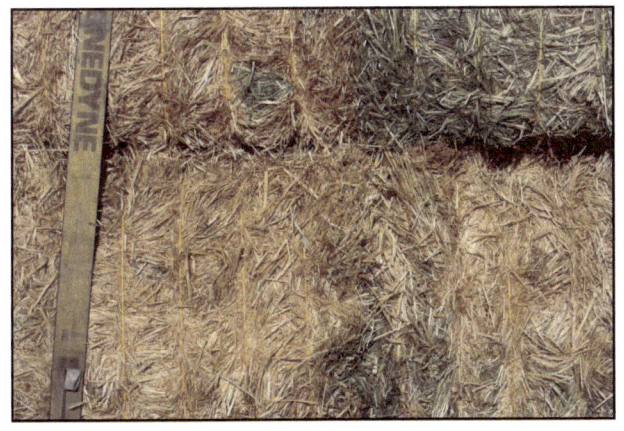

Endangered
Photos:
Hay Bales
#162

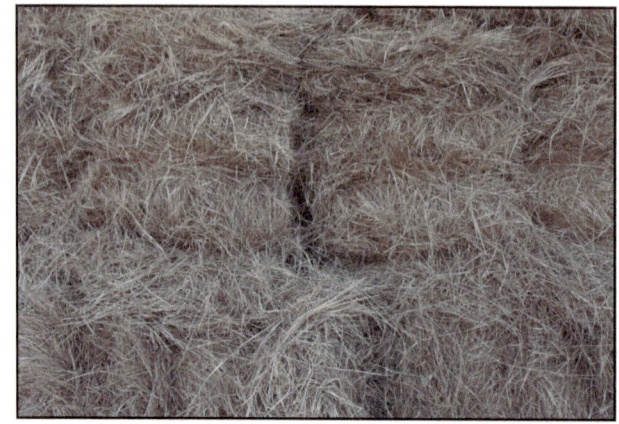

Endangered
Photos:
Hay Bales
#163

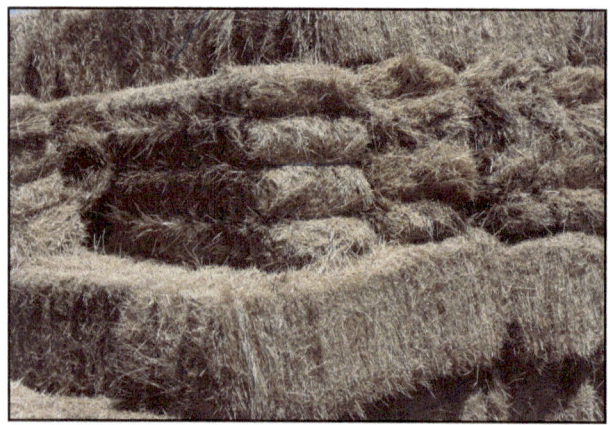

Endangered
Photos:
Hay Bales
#164

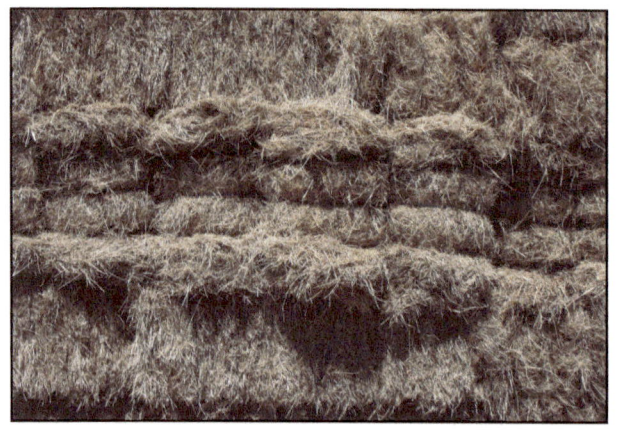

Endangered
Photos:
Hay Bales
#165

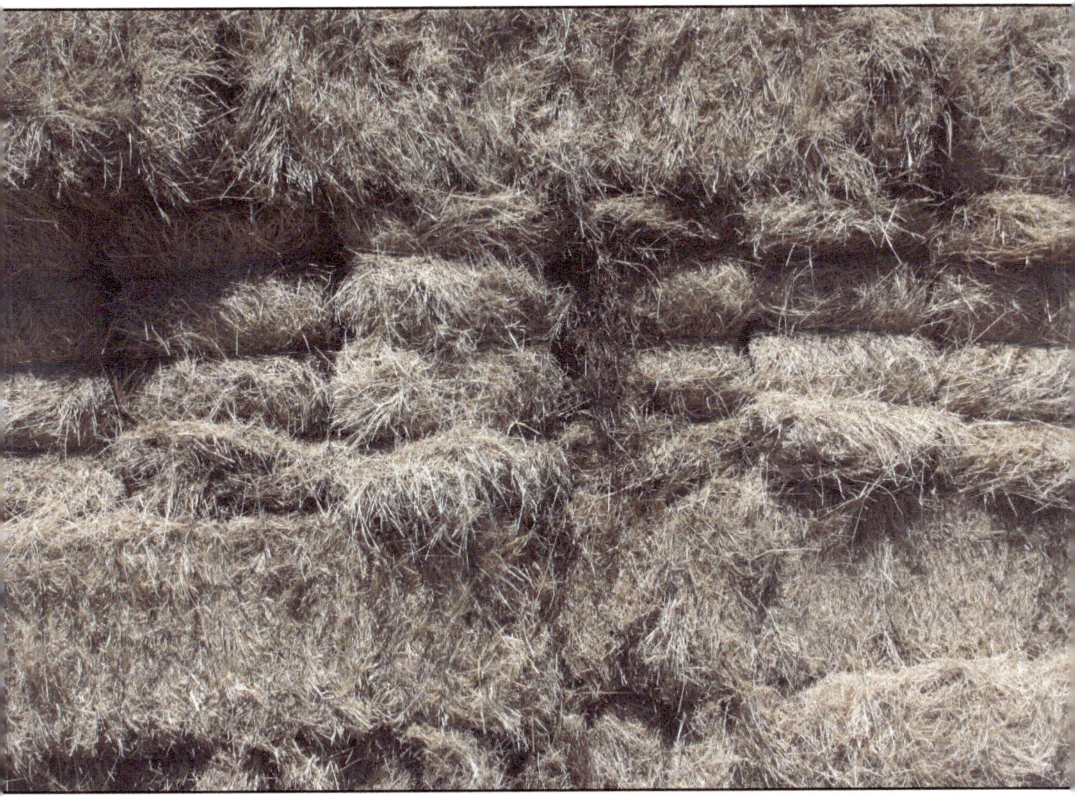

Endangered Photos: Hay Bales #166

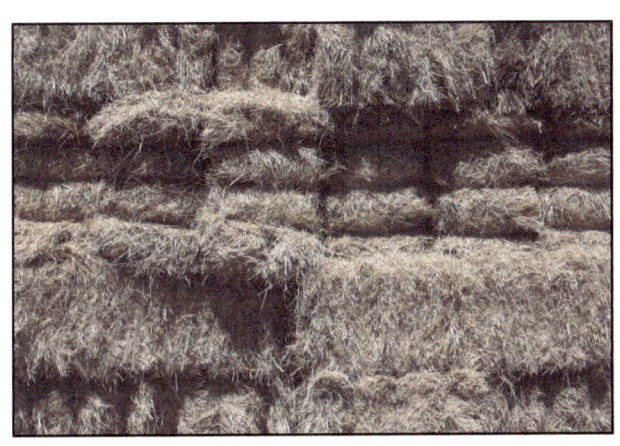

Endangered Photos: Hay Bales #167

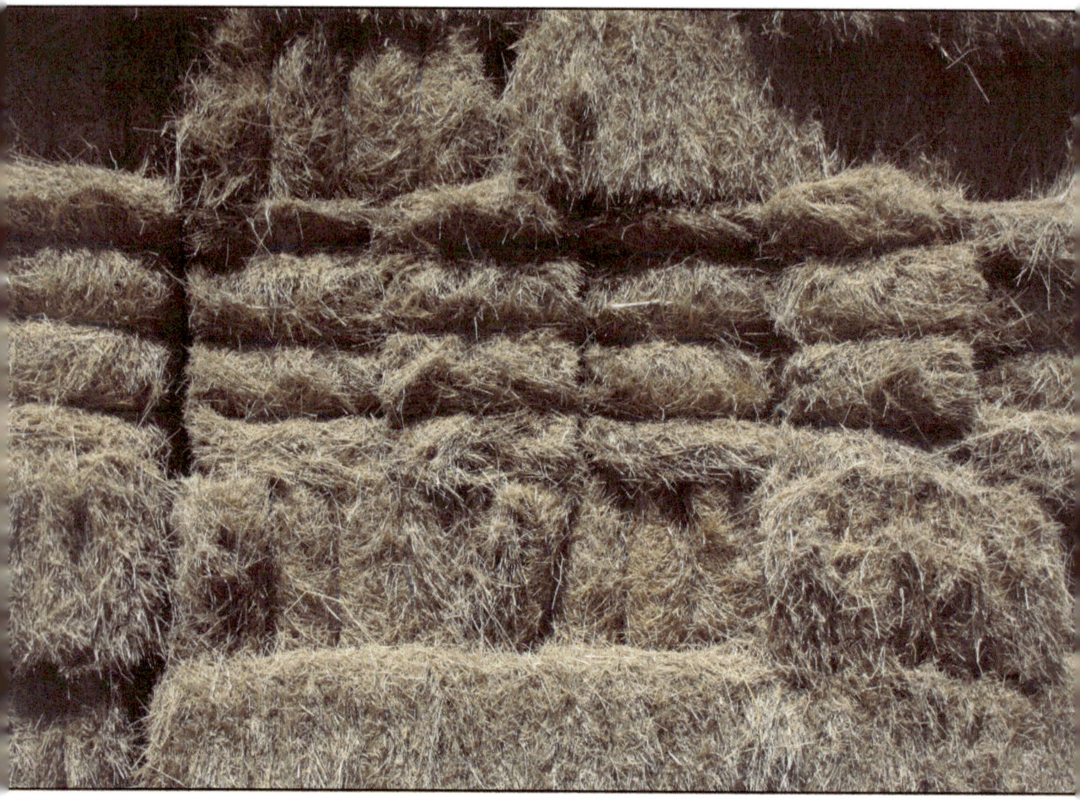

Endangered Photos: Hay Bales #168

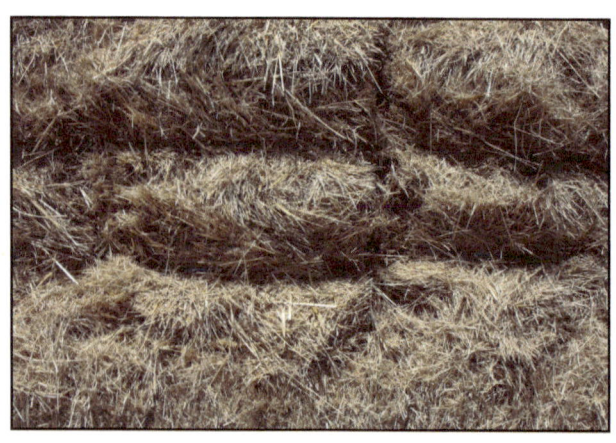

Endangered
Photos:
Hay Bales
#169

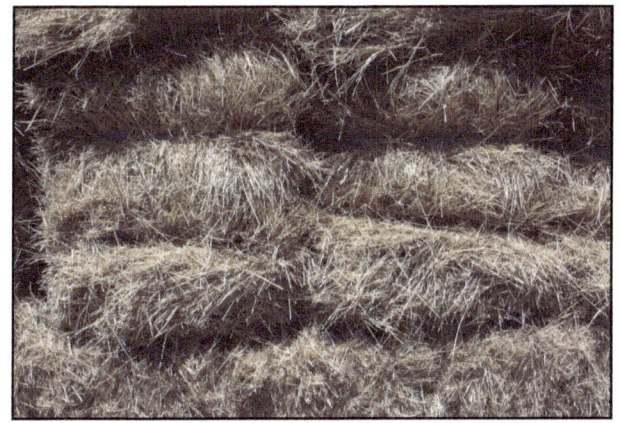

Endangered
Photos:
Hay Bales
#170

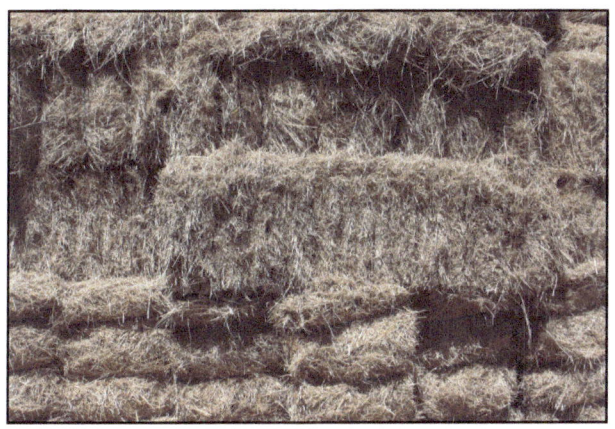

Endangered
Photos:
Hay Bales
#171

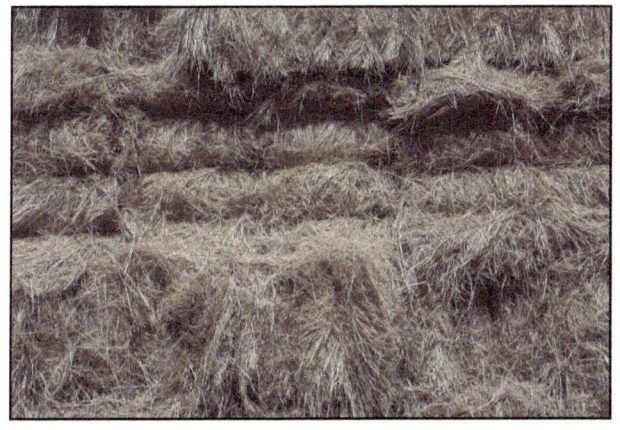

Endangered
Photos:
Hay Bales
#172

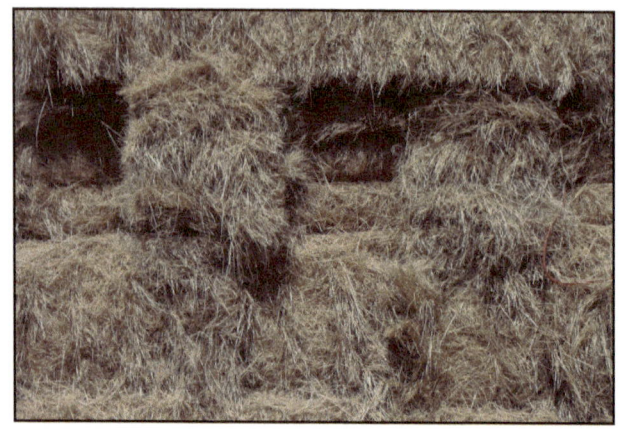

Endangered
Photos:
Hay Bales
#173

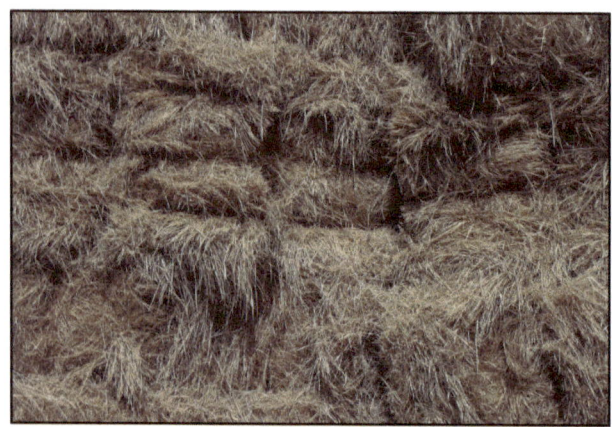

Endangered
Photos:
Hay Bales
#174

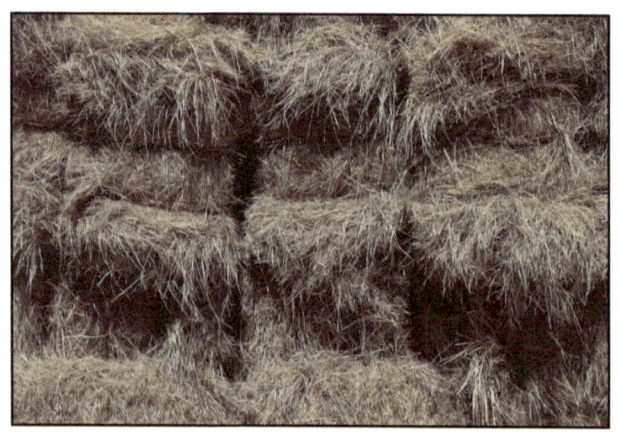

Endangered
Photos:
Hay Bales
#175

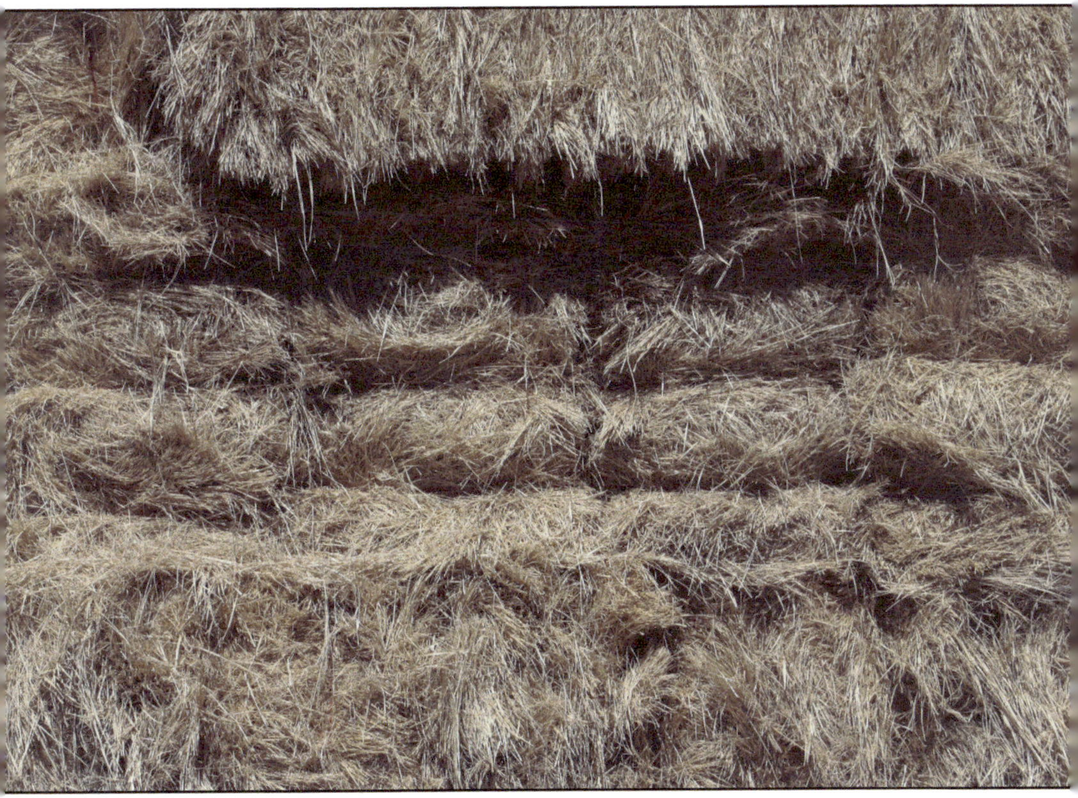

Endangered Photos: Hay Bales #176

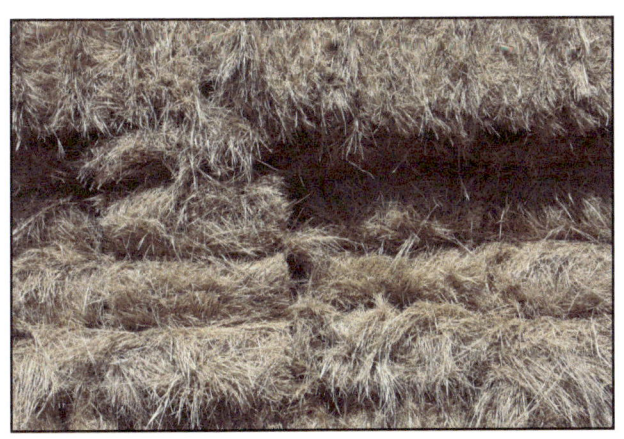

Endangered Photos: Hay Bales #177

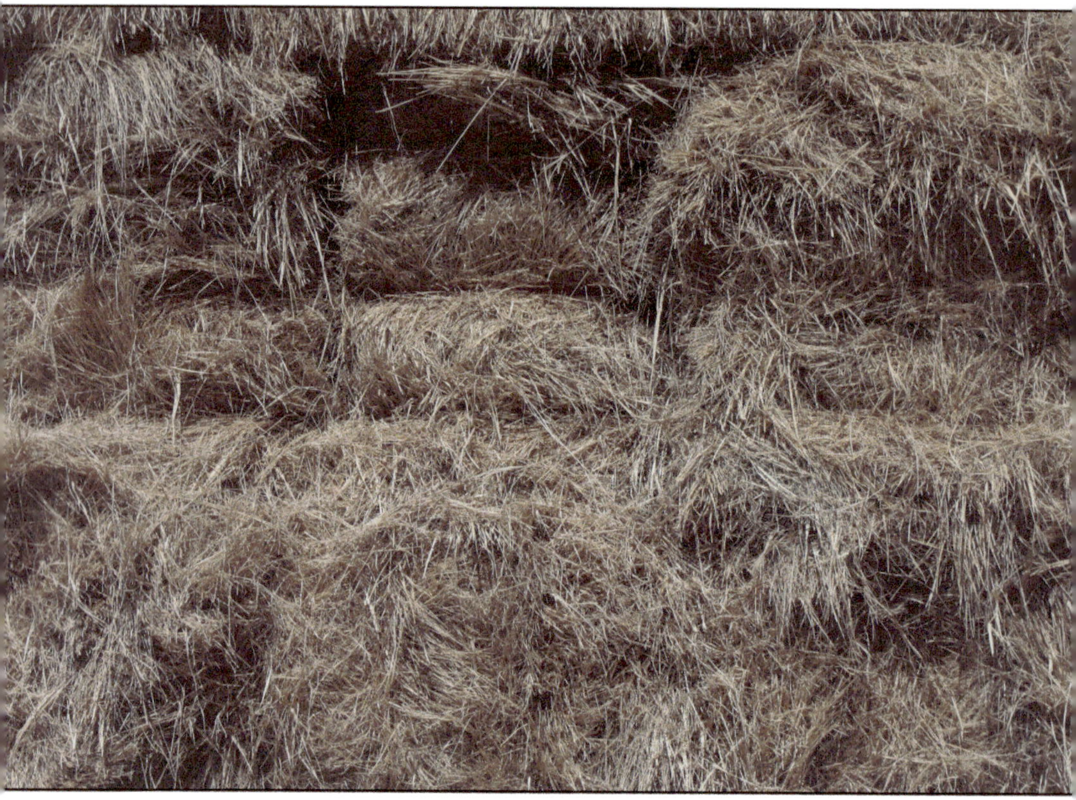

Endangered Photos: Hay Bales #178

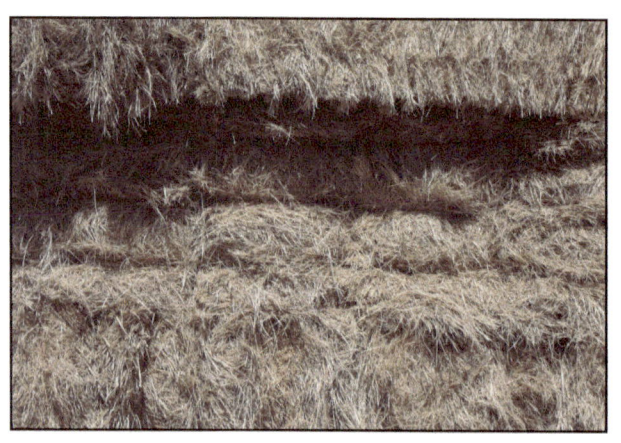

Endangered Photos: Hay Bales #179

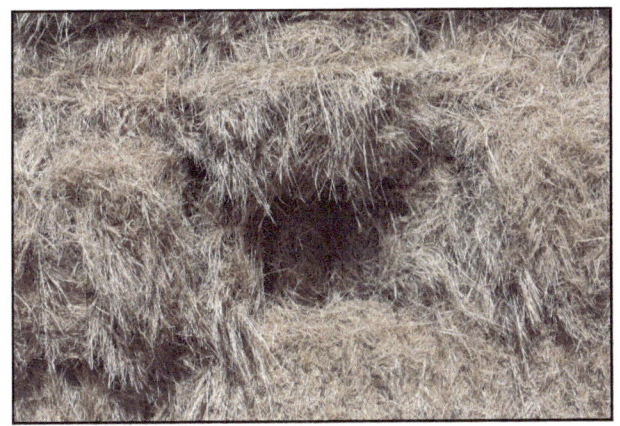

Endangered
Photos:
Hay Bales
#180

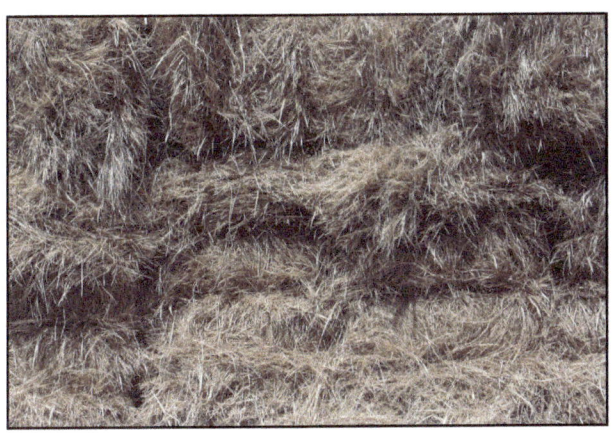

Endangered
Photos:
Hay Bales
#181

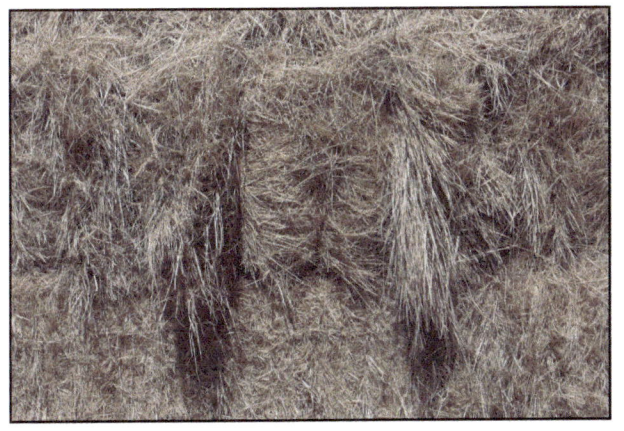

Endangered
Photos:
Hay Bales
#182

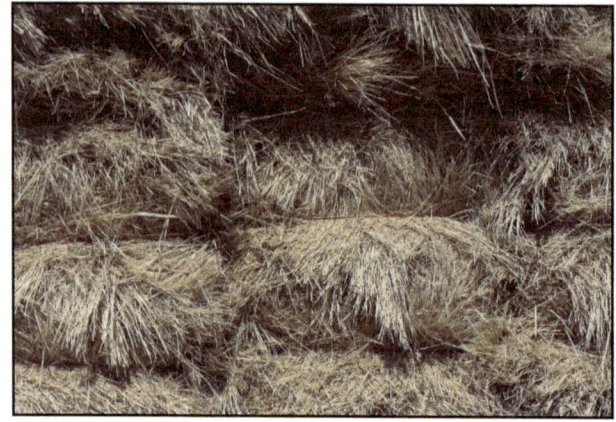

Endangered
Photos:
Hay Bales
#183

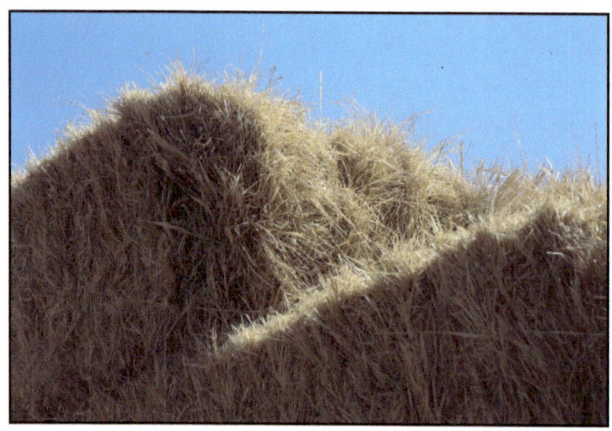

Endangered
Photos:
Hay Bales
#184

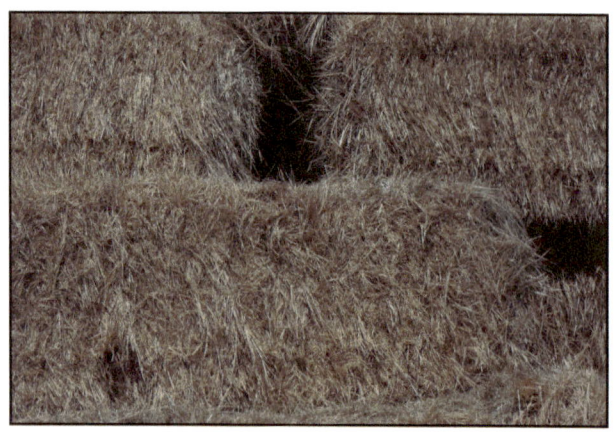

Endangered
Photos:
Hay Bales
#185

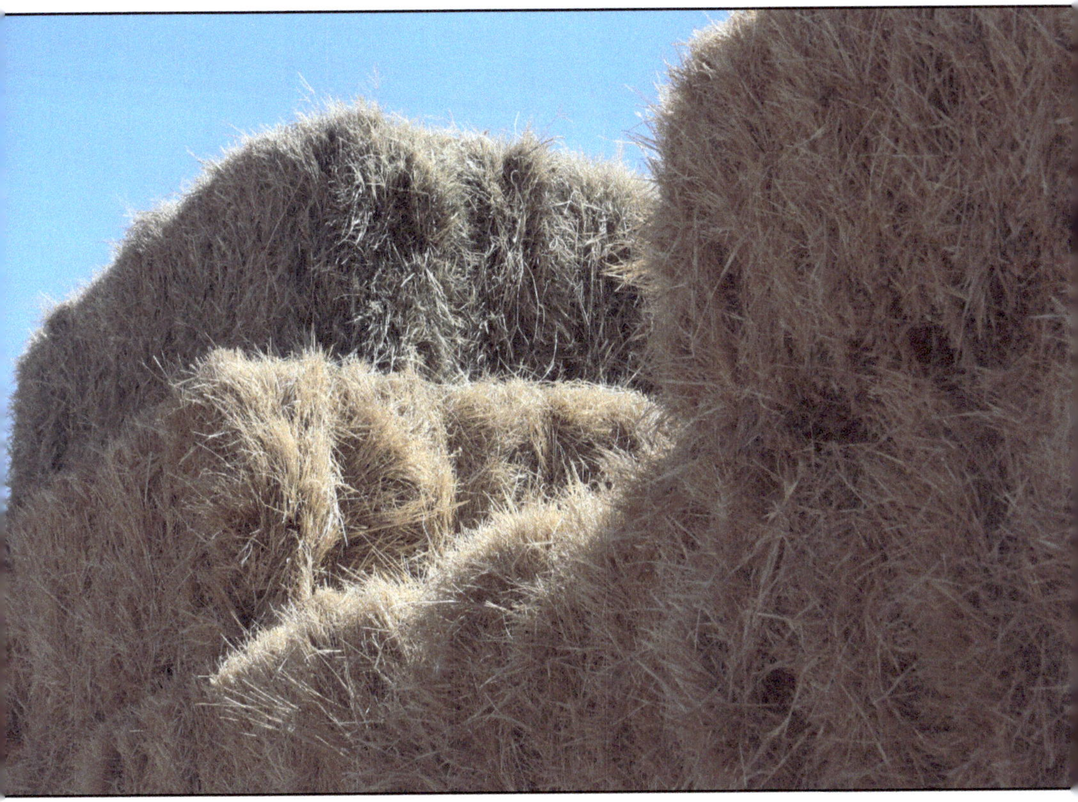

Endangered Photos: Hay Bales #186

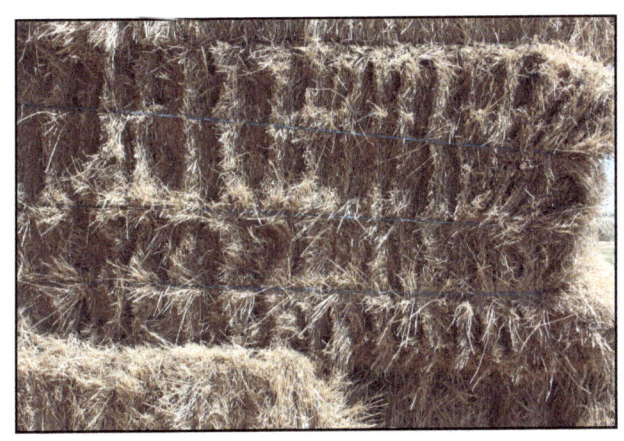

Endangered Photos: Hay Bales #187

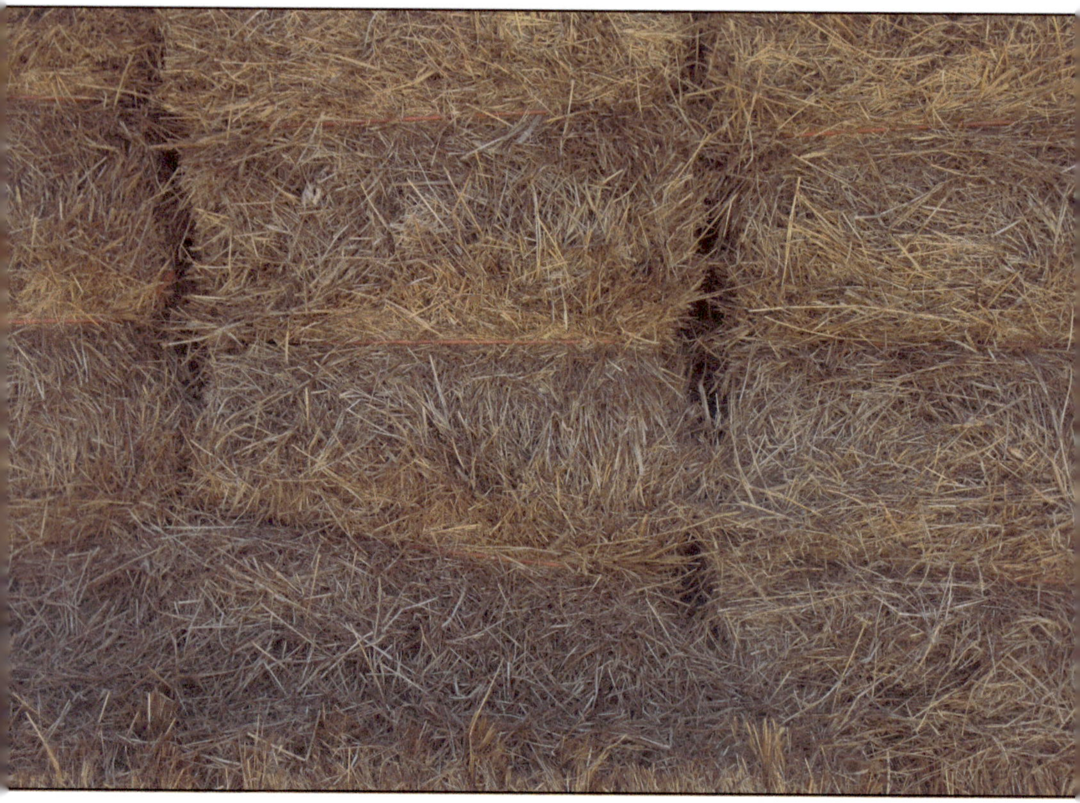

Endangered Photos: Hay Bales #188

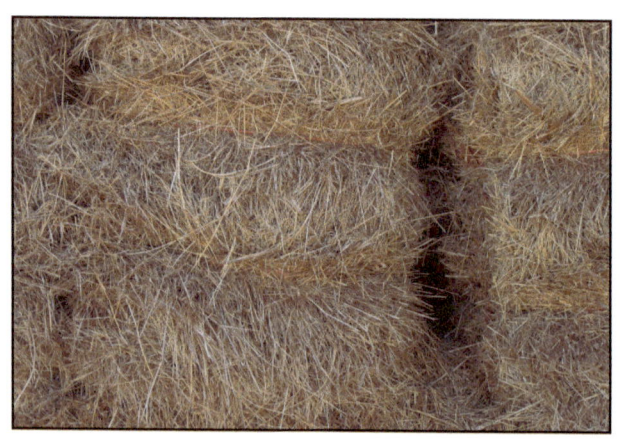

Endangered Photos: Hay Bales #189

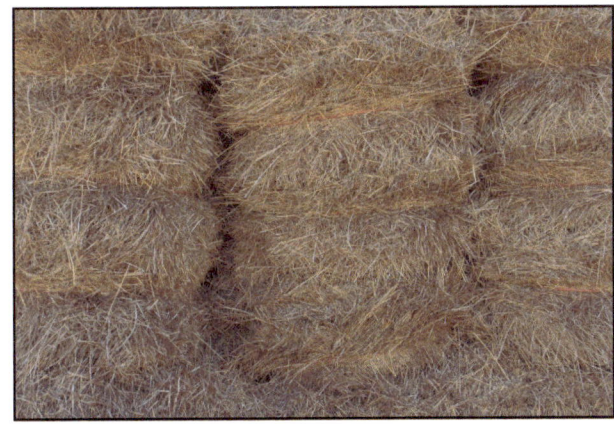

Endangered
Photos:
Hay Bales
#190

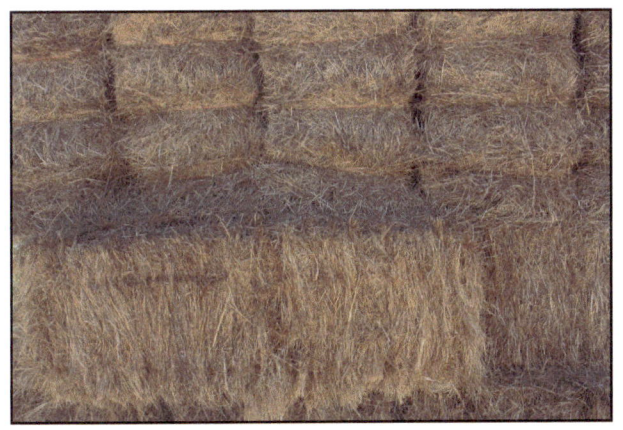

Endangered
Photos:
Hay Bales
#191

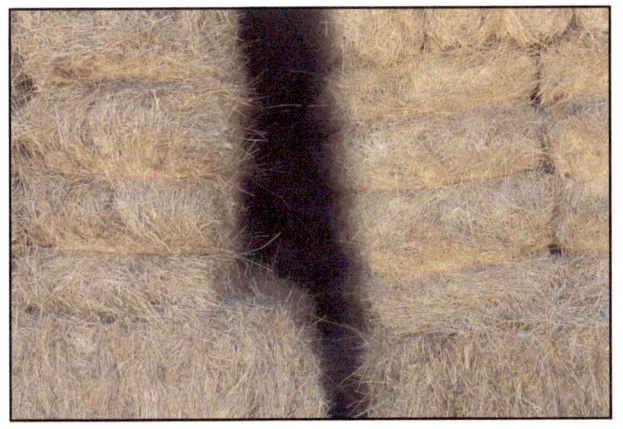

Endangered
Photos:
Hay Bales
#192

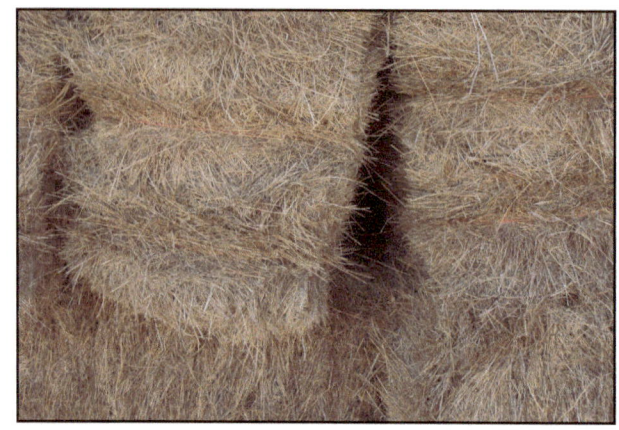

Endangered Photos: Hay Bales #193

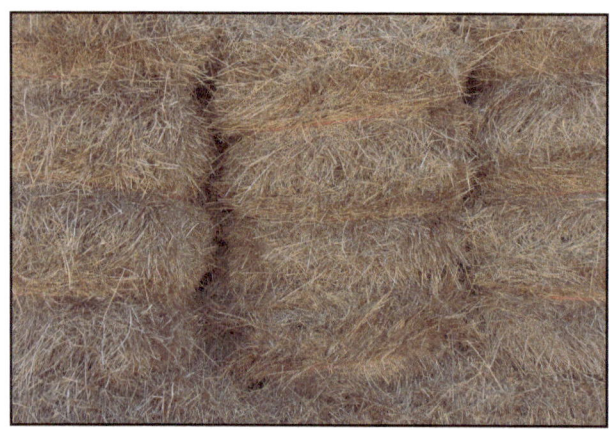

Endangered Photos: Hay Bales #194

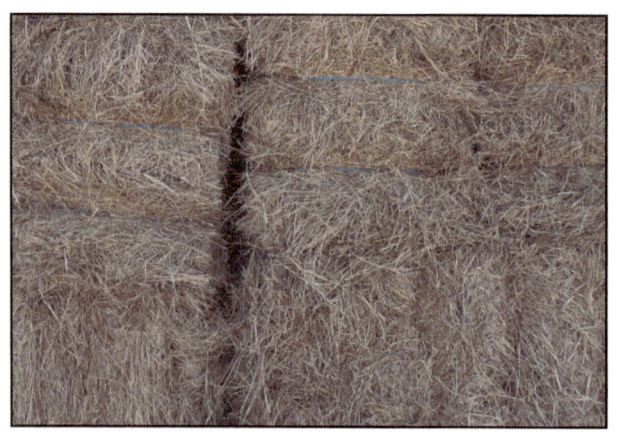

Endangered Photos: Hay Bales #195

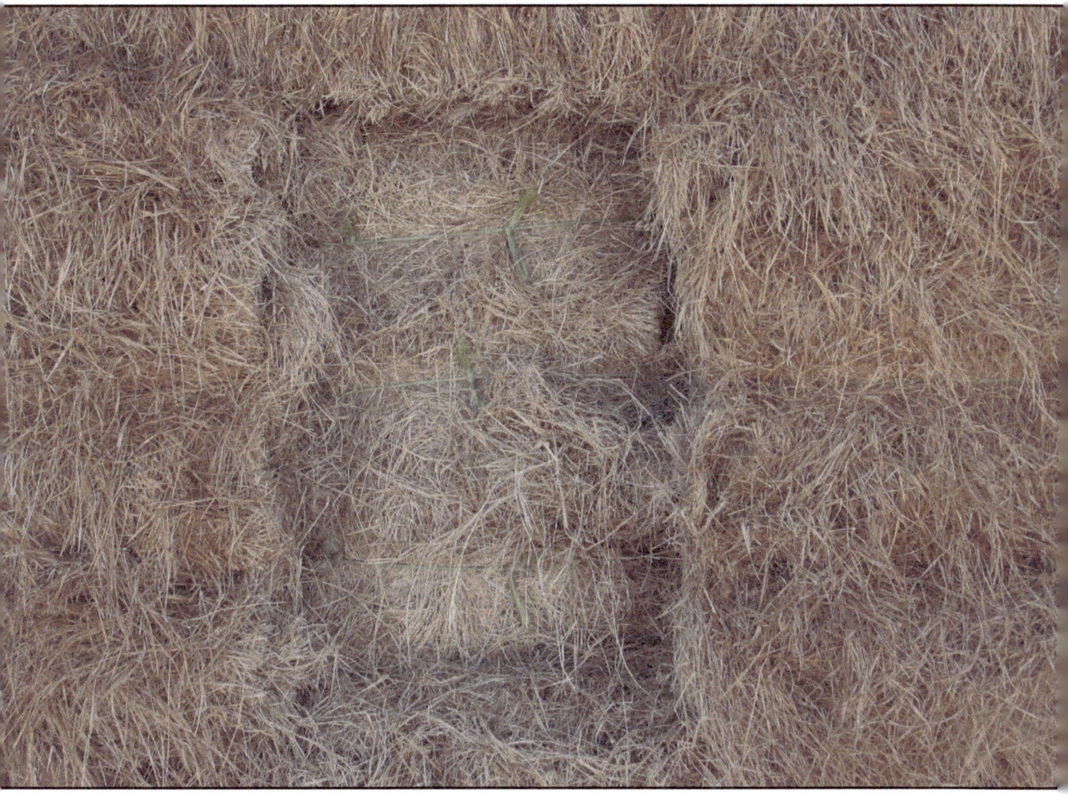

Endangered Photos: Hay Bales #196

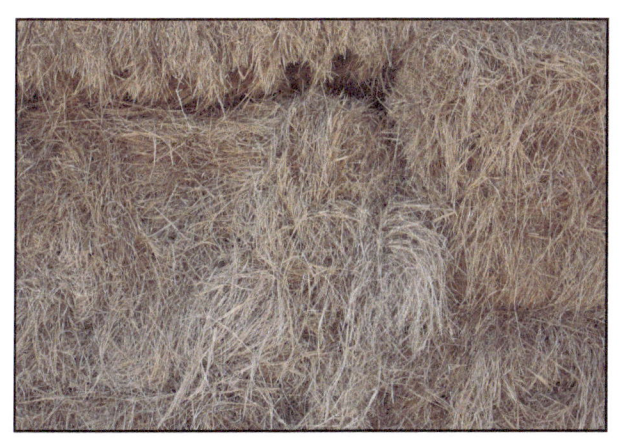

Endangered Photos: Hay Bales #197

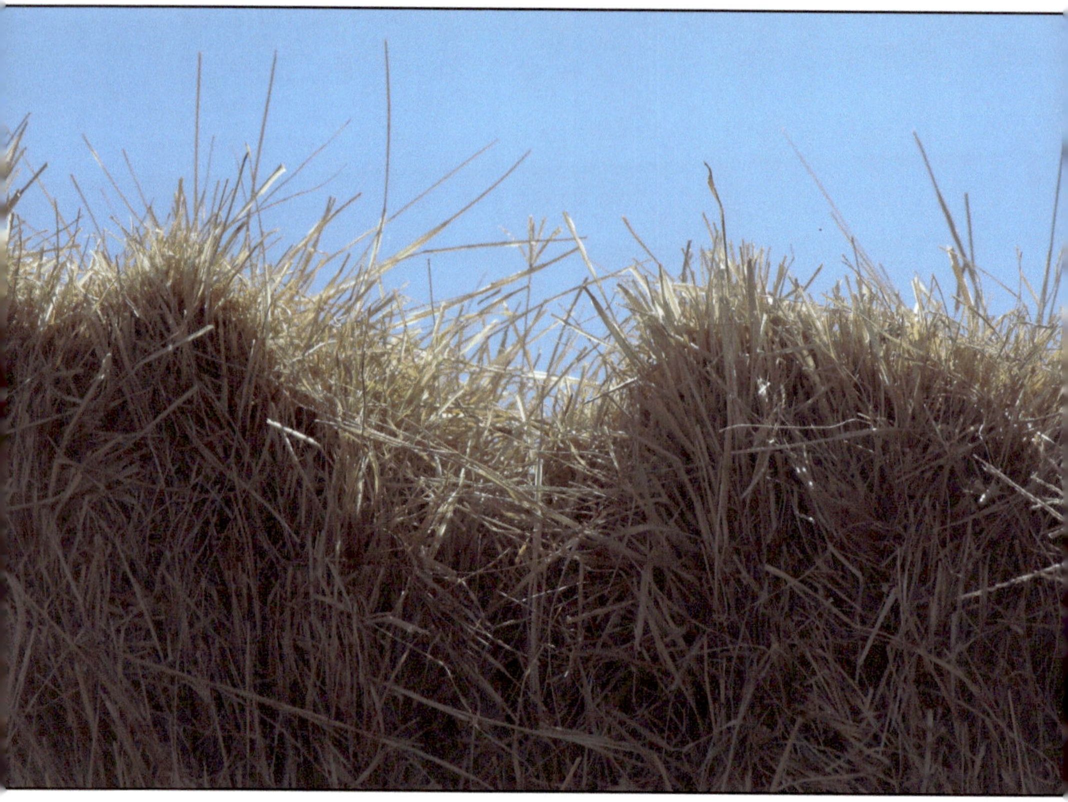

Endangered Photos: Hay Bales #198

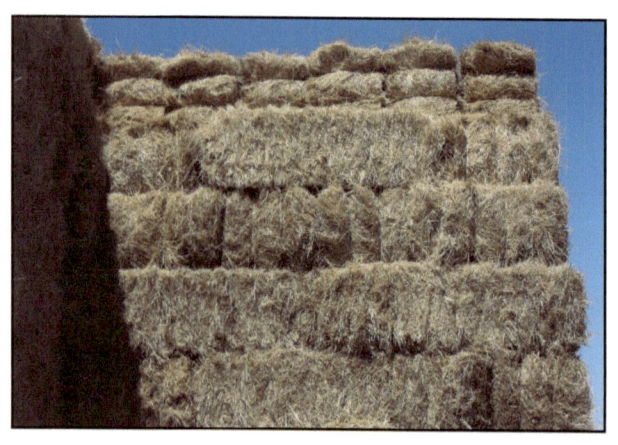

Endangered
Photos:
Hay Bales
#199

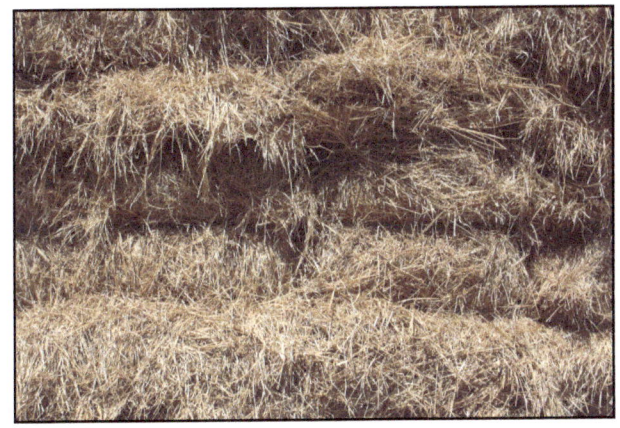

Endangered
Photos:
Hay Bales
#200

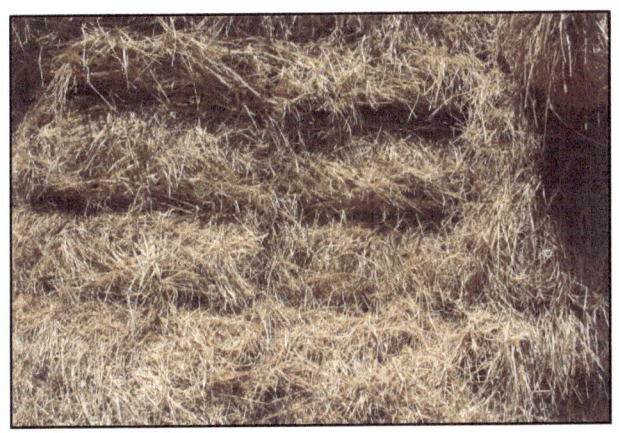

Endangered
Photos:
Hay Bales
#201

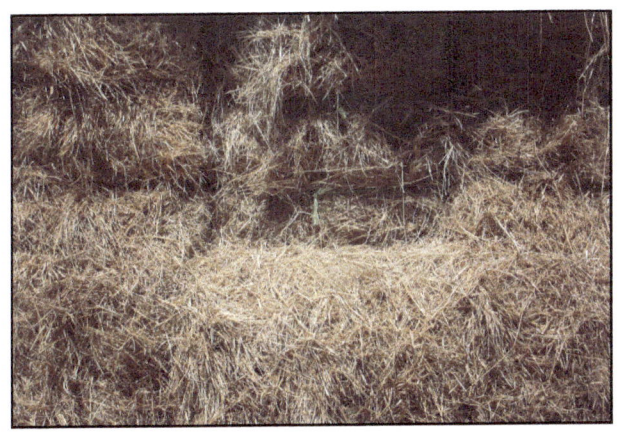

Endangered
Photos:
Hay Bales
#202

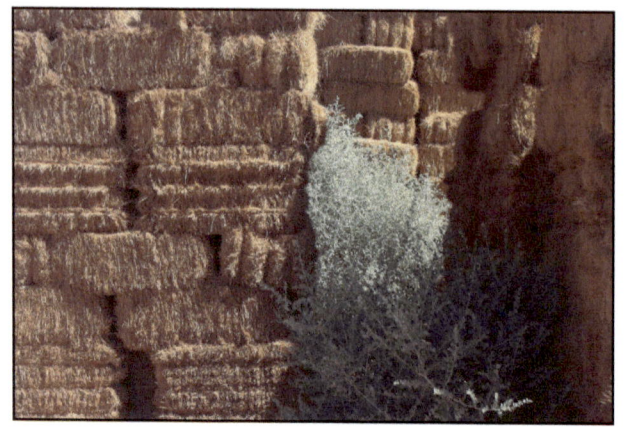

Endangered
Photos:
Hay Bales
#203

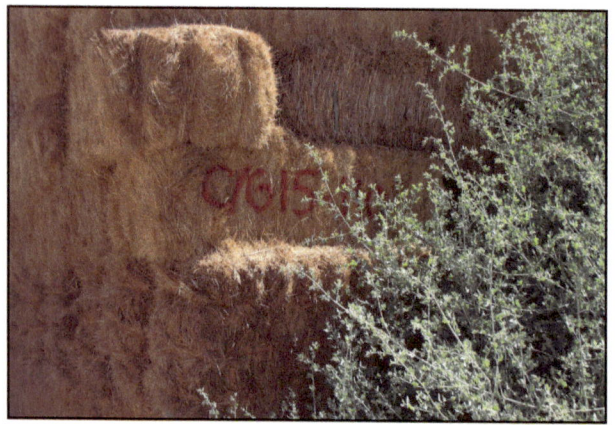

Endangered
Photos:
Hay Bales
#204

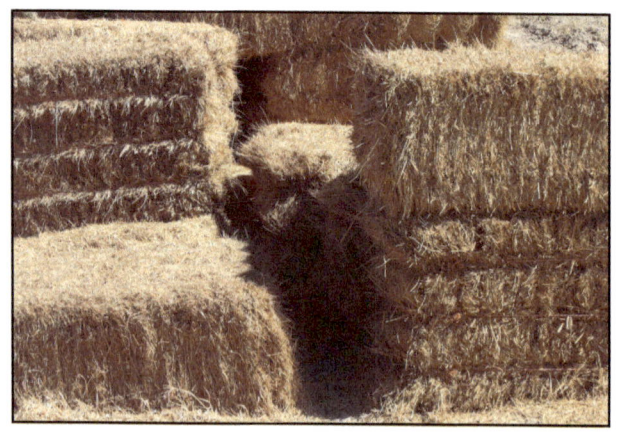

Endangered
Photos:
Hay Bales
#205

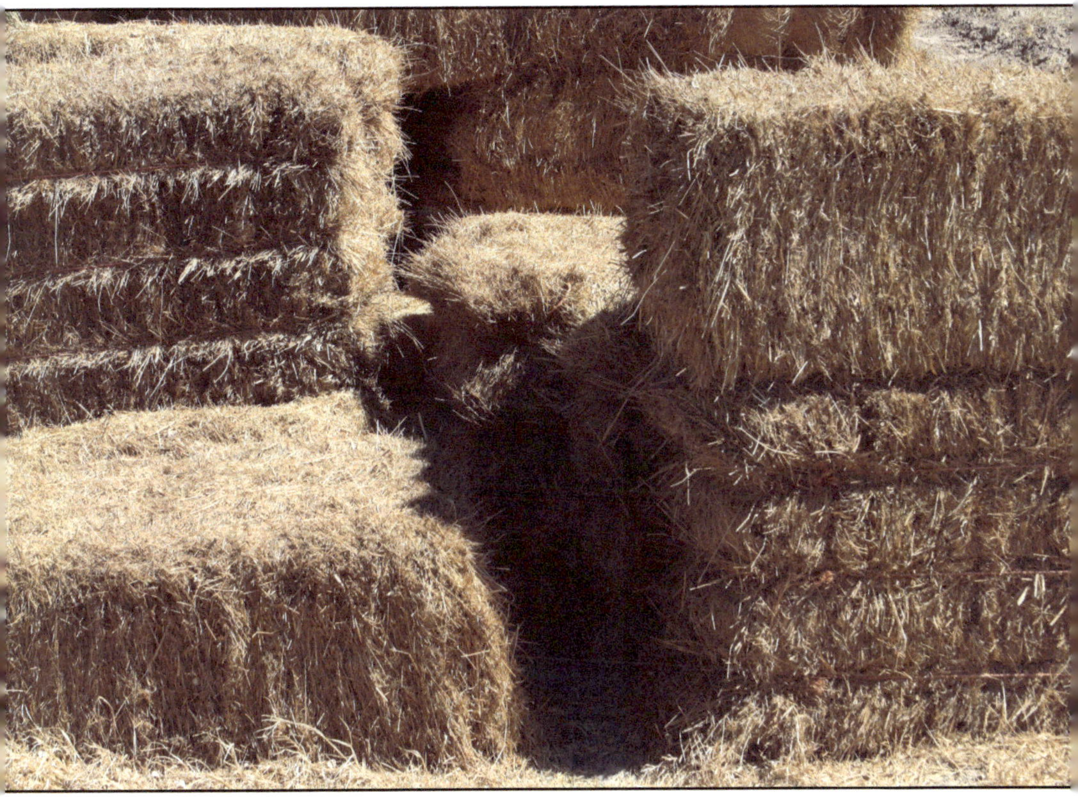

Endangered Photos: Hay Bales #206

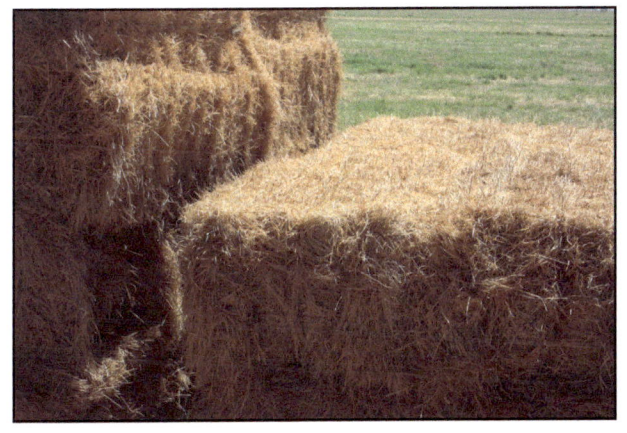

Endangered Photos: Hay Bales #207

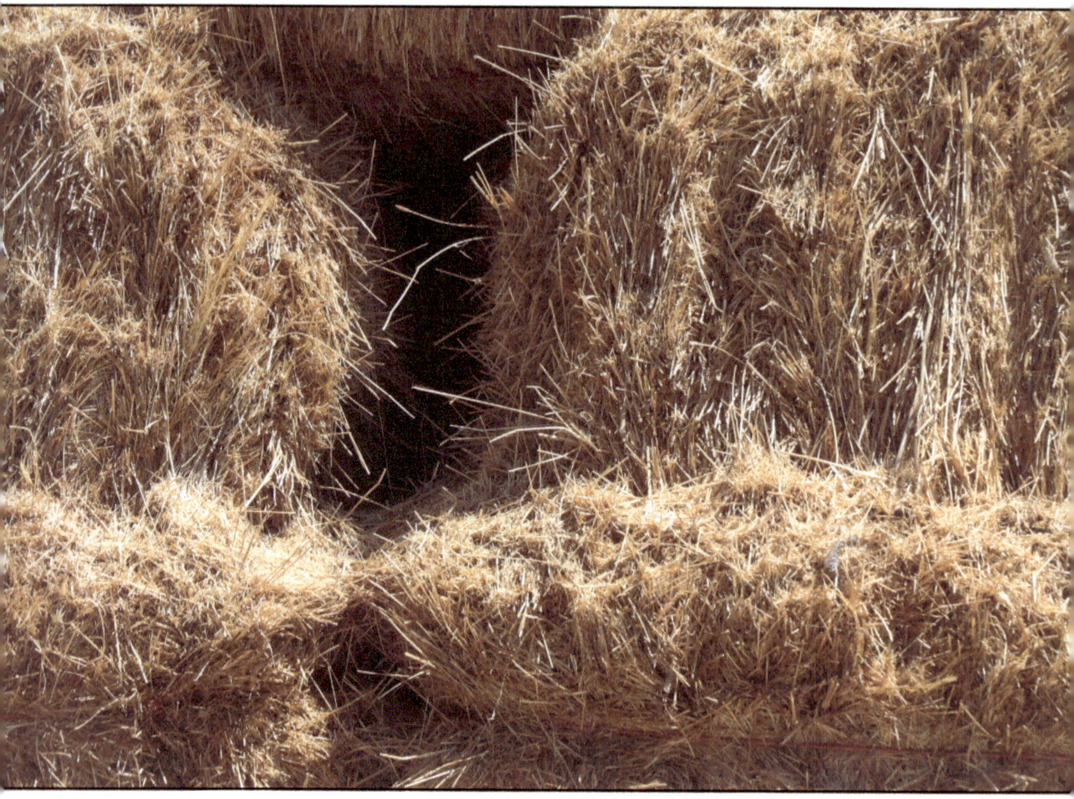

Endangered Photos: Hay Bales #208

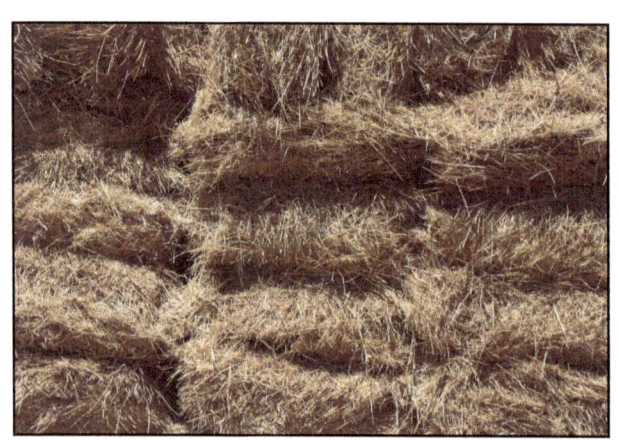

Endangered Photos: Hay Bales #209

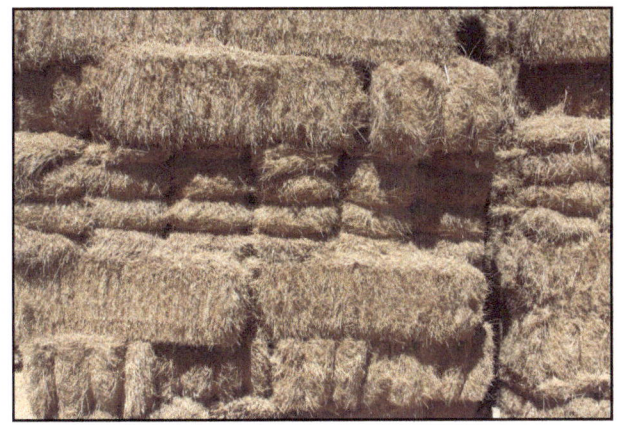

Endangered
Photos:
Hay Bales
#210

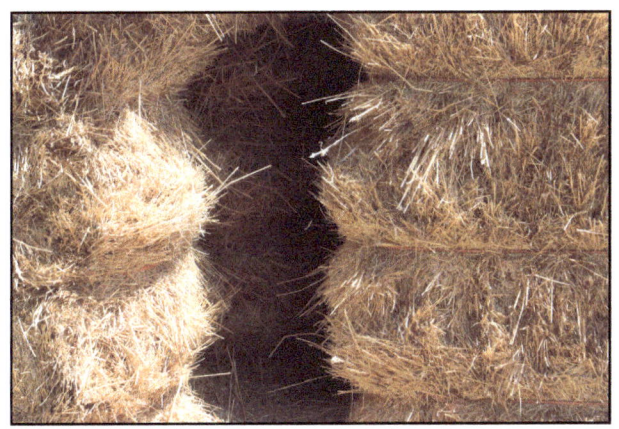

Endangered
Photos:
Hay Bales
#211

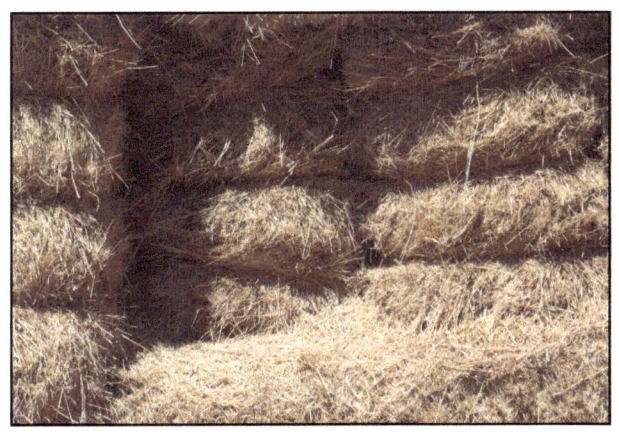

Endangered
Photos:
Hay Bales
#212

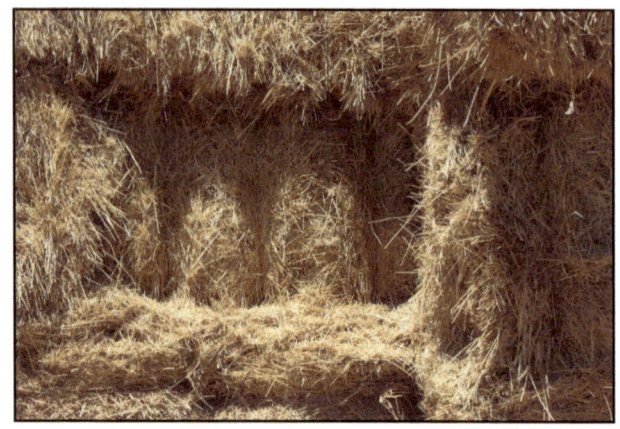

Endangered
Photos:
Hay Bales
#213

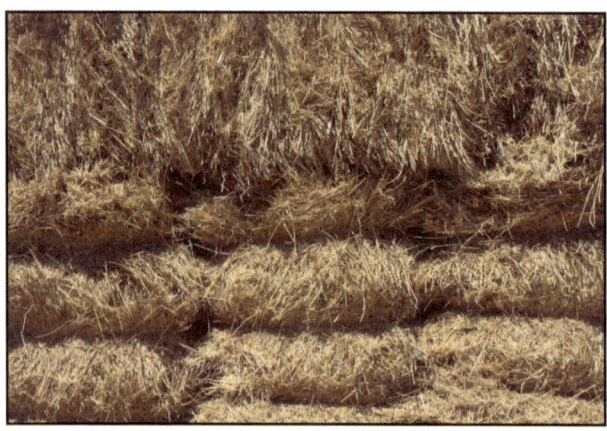

Endangered
Photos:
Hay Bales
#214

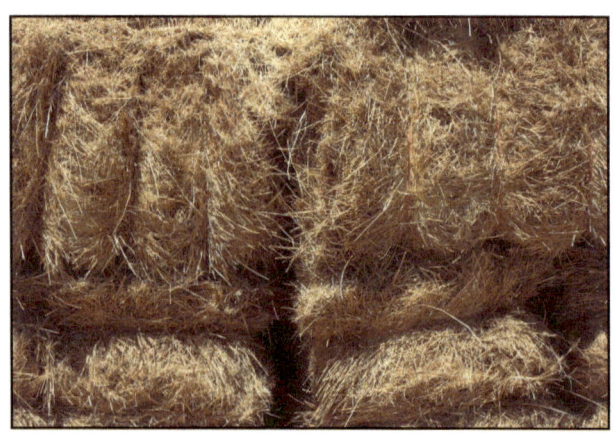

Endangered
Photos:
Hay Bales
#215

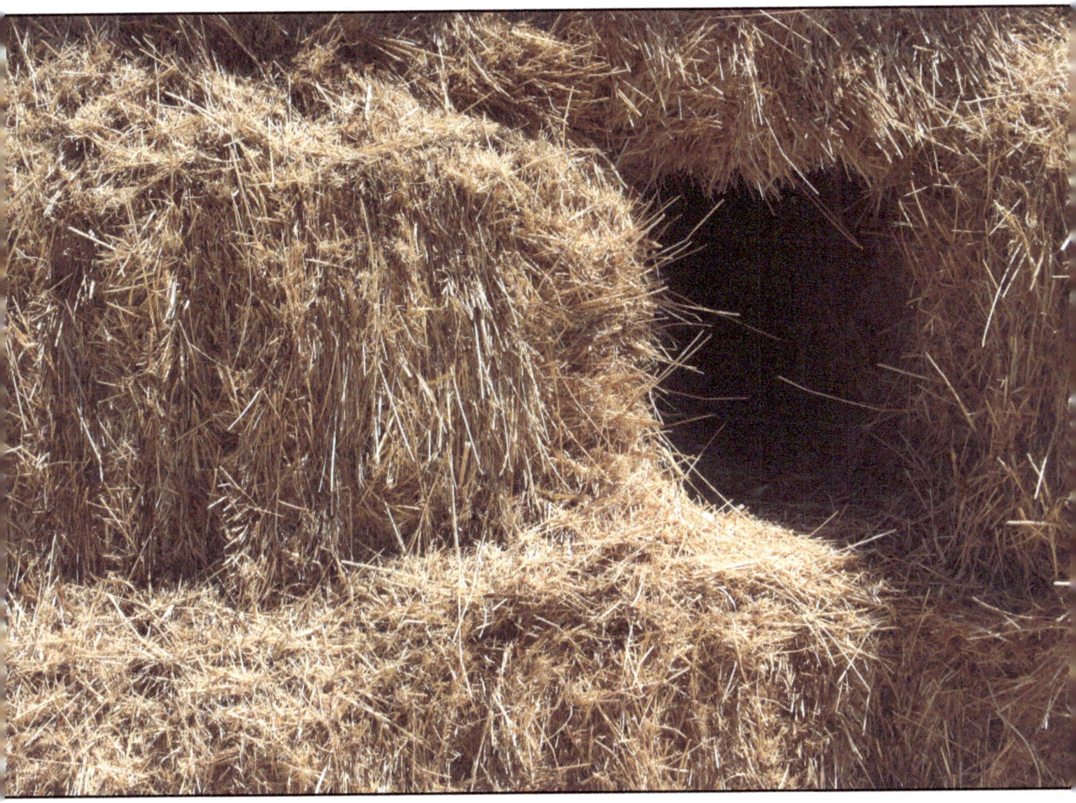

Endangered Photos: Hay Bales #216

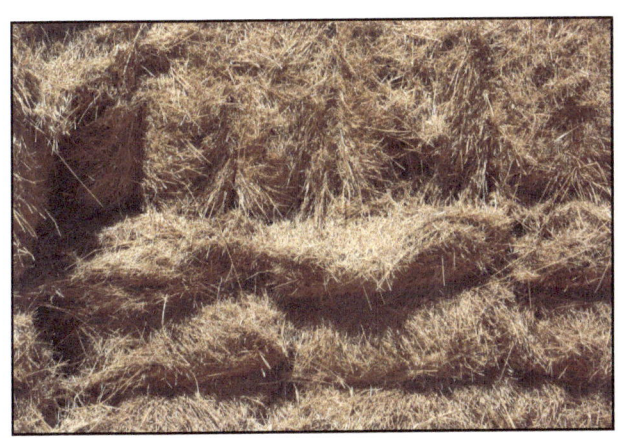

Endangered
Photos:
Hay Bales
#217

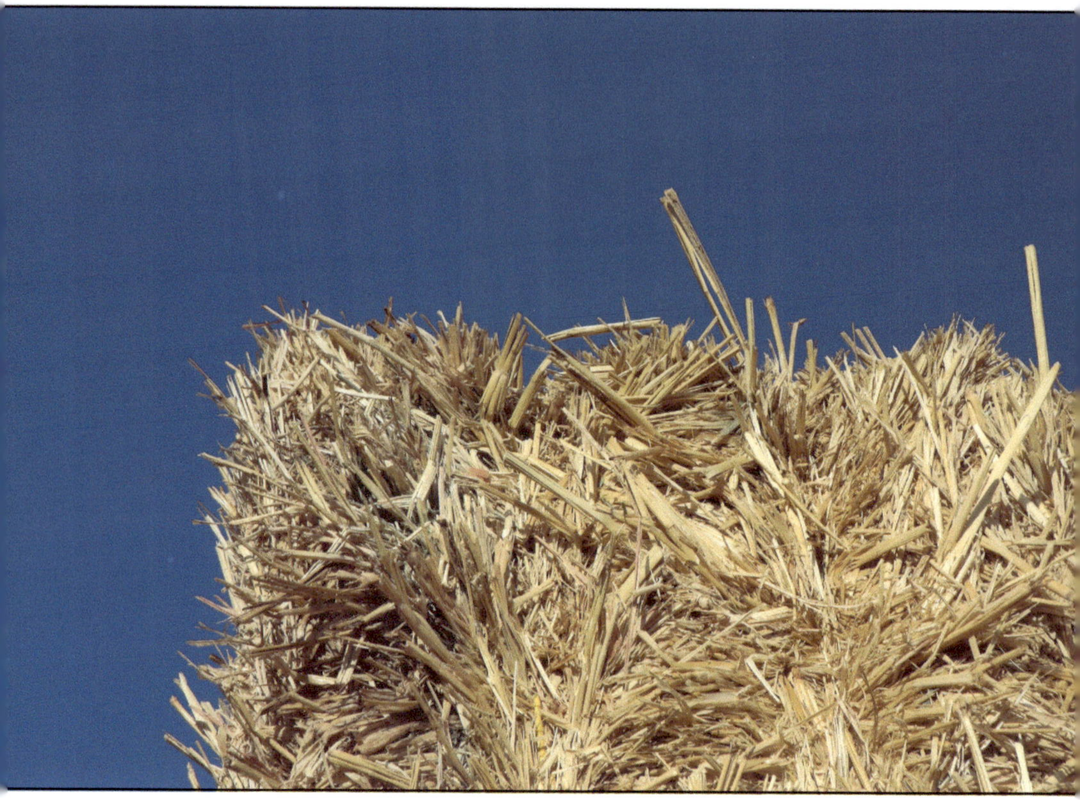

Endangered Photos: Hay Bales #218

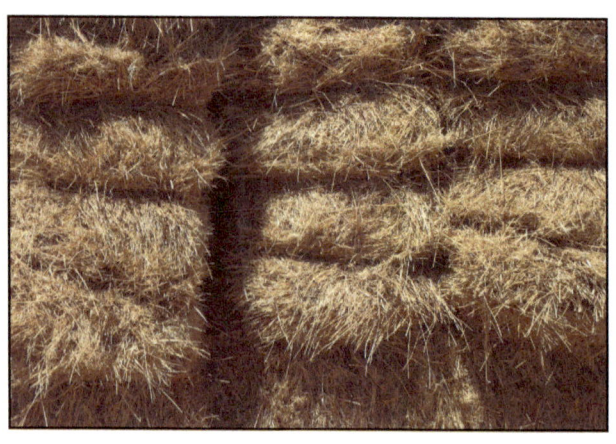

Endangered Photos: Hay Bales #219

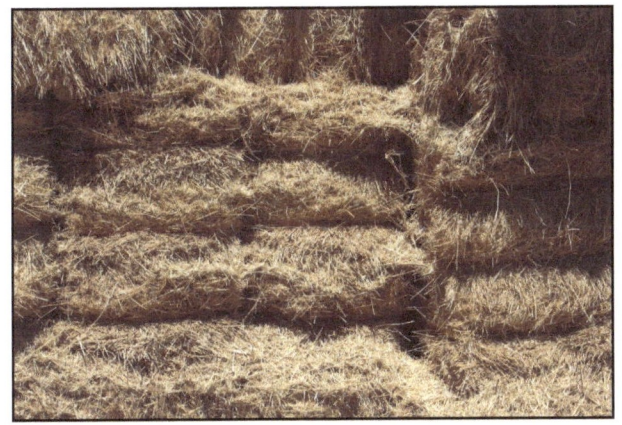

Endangered
Photos:
Hay Bales
#220

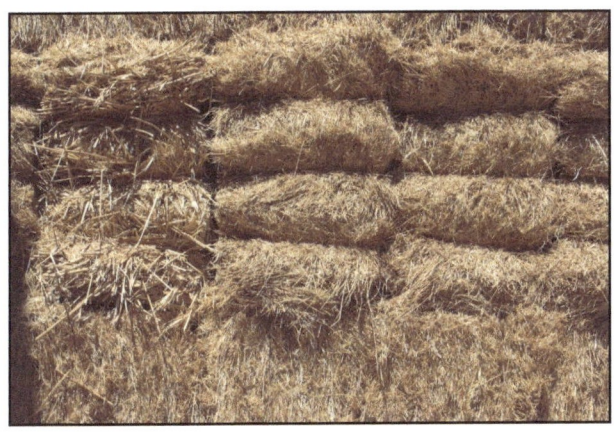

Endangered
Photos:
Hay Bales
#221

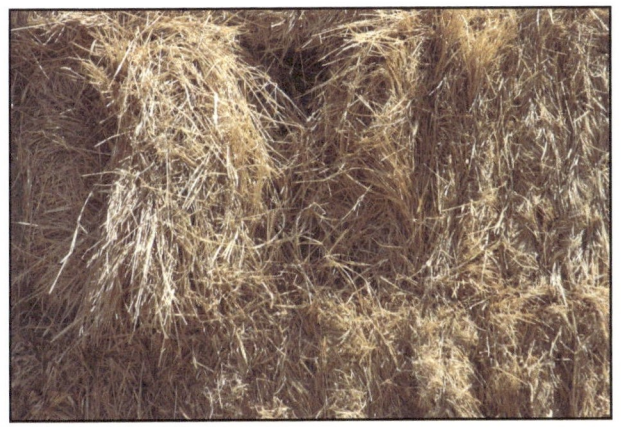

Endangered
Photos:
Hay Bales
#222

A Mark Dahle Portfolio

Endangered Photos

Train Cars #112-222

This Mark Dahle Portfolio includes a colorful painting, a brief description of the *Endangered Photos* project and 111 beautiful photographs from Mark Dahle's *Endangered Photos* series.

Images in Mark Dahle's series of *Endangered Photos* are one-of-a-kind originals. Only one print is made by Mark Dahle from each image.

A Mark Dahle Portfolio

Endangered Photos

Telephone Poles #112-222

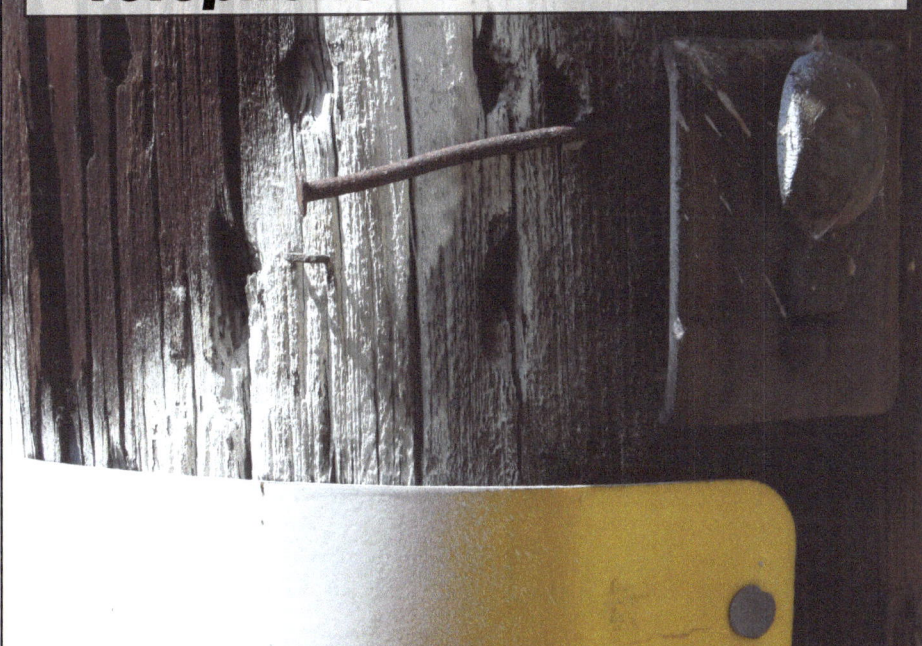

This Mark Dahle Portfolio includes a colorful painting, a brief description of the Endangered Photos *project*, and 111 beautiful photographs of telephone poles from Mark Dahle's series of Endangered Photos.

Unlike most fine art photographs where multiple prints exist, images in Mark Dahle's series of *Endangered Photos* are one-of-a-kind originals. . . . If anything happens to the artwork, it is lost forever.

A Mark Dahle Portfolio

Endangered Photos

Railroad Ties #112-222

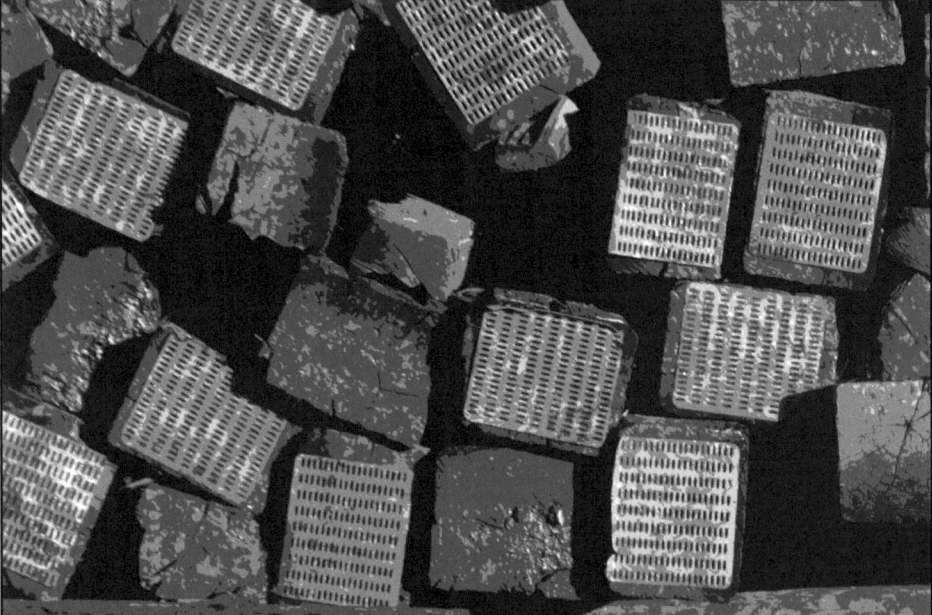

This Mark Dahle Portfolio includes a colorful painting, a brief description of the Endangered Photos *project* and 111 beautiful photographs from Mark Dahle's Endangered Photos *series.*

The beauty that surrounds us (often unnoticed) is to be appreciated in this moment. . . . What we have an opportunity to notice today is only available today.

www.ingramcontent.com/pod-product-compliance
Lightning Source LLC
Chambersburg PA
CBHW040243220526
45473CB00001B/351